Praise for Al

"All Hands: The Evolution of a Volunteer Disaster Response Organization is the story of how David Campbell grew from technology executive to Purpose-Prize-winning philanthropist. It's a great read!"

—Robert E. Cook, author of Pulse and Bairdston (a young adult novel), Robert E. Honors College benefactor and activist, and former CEO of NYSE technology company

"David Campbell's account of disaster response—from Thailand to Mississippi, Haiti to Nepal—demonstrates that we each have the power to save a life and rebuild a community if we join our hands together. With excruciating honesty, Campbell describes what it takes to build a volunteer team that is flexible, efficient, and respectful of the local culture, while building an organization that is sustainable through one unpredictable crisis to another. At once business entrepreneur and social entrepreneur, Campbell epitomizes adaptive—just the kind we need to transform global disasters into opportunities for renewal, for both volunteers and the communities they serve."

—Karen Keating Ansara, Director, Ansara Family Foundation

"In researching ways we could connect with the community, All Hands Volunteers—a grass roots organization that was connecting with the communities it was trying to help—was at the top of my list. All Hands Volunteers is an "all are welcome" organization and that's special. It allows people to get in where they fit in."

—Sara Bareilles, five-time Grammy nominated singer/songwriter and All Hands volunteer

"While the disaster response sector is slowly moving toward building the capacity of local actors, there will always be events that simply overwhelm local structures. David Campbell has held together an organization that, uniquely, puts things in place to allow unpaid volunteers to help distressed communities as they work to get back on their feet."

—Kenny Rae, Disaster Response Specialist, Oxfam America

The EVOLUTION of a VOLUNTEER-POWERED
DISASTER RESPONSE ORGANIZATION

ALL HANDS

David Campbell with Catherine Fredman

RIVER GROVE
BOOKS

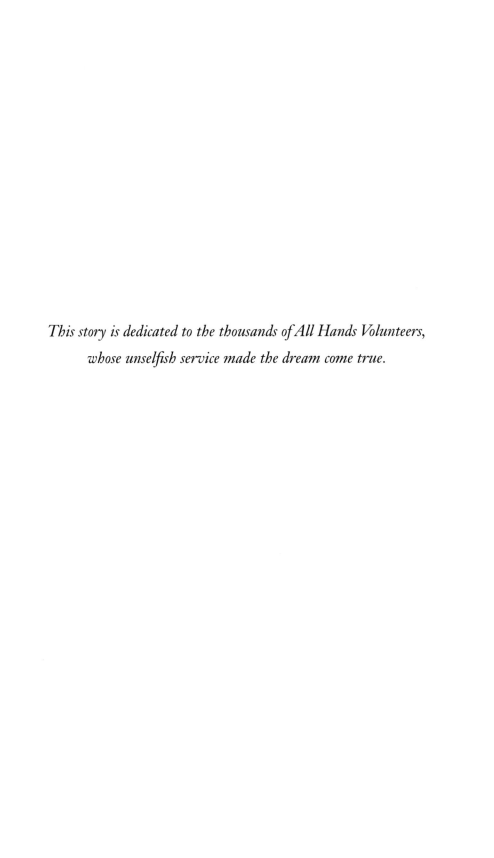

This story is dedicated to the thousands of All Hands Volunteers,
whose unselfish service made the dream come true.

Published by River Grove Books
Austin, TX
www.rivergrovebooks.com

Distributed by River Grove Books

For ordering information or special discounts for bulk purchases, please contact River Grove Books at PO Box 91869, Austin, TX 78709, 512-891-6100.

Design and composition by Greenleaf Book Group
Cover design by Greenleaf Book Group
Cover photograph and interior photographs by Gay Wind Campbell©

Cataloging-in-Publication Data is available.

ISBN: 978-1-63299-062-4

eBook ISBN: 978-1-63299-063-1

First Edition

Contents

Foreword

We live in a giving America. When disaster strikes, no matter where in the world, Americans respond with offers of help. Disaster pulls at our heartstrings, and there is an overwhelming urge to take action. So, what happened when a retired technology executive from Boston decided to answer the call to action and respond to the tsunami that hit Thailand in 2004? Well, he rolled up his sleeves and got involved, of course.

Meet David Campbell, founder and creator of All Hands Volunteers. Remembering his call to action after the tsunami of 2004, he told me, "I didn't know disaster relief, but I knew technology, and I just knew that I had something to offer the people of Thailand who had just lost everything." *All Hands: The Evolution of a Volunteer-Powered Disaster Response Organization* will show you how David and his volunteers came together to make a difference.

David has written a practical and heartwarming book in which he shares the how-to of disaster relief and tells us what it is like for a volunteer to be on the ground at the outset of relief efforts. He conveys how surprised he is by the numbers of volunteers who travel from all over the world to help All Hands Volunteers, and he shares unexpected surprises at each site that will make you believe in the good of people and the magic of helping others. David's stories will remind you that when we come together, our hands have the ability to help, to heal, and to give back.

When I first met David two years ago, I was immediately struck by what he and All Hands Volunteers had accomplished. I knew very little about disaster relief. David shared his stories with me—passionately telling me how rewarding it is to not only volunteer but also to know that each of us has the power to touch a life that has taken an unexpected hit. The stories that David shared with me two years ago are now here, in *All Hands*, for you to enjoy.

The stories and the good works of All Hands Volunteers will make you feel special, whether you're pounding nails on a job site or writing a check. They do an impressive job of keeping donors engaged in what's happening and whom they are helping. They communicate the astonishing stories of the families. It's all part of the All Hands magic, that euphoric feeling that sticks with you—that giving is good and you did something to help.

David changed my perception of disaster relief organizations by showing me that there are great people giving their time and talent— great people like those who have joined the All Hands Volunteers family. That's why this book is so important to me and why it is a must read for anyone who wants to help when there's a natural disaster.

The stories in this book will inspire you. They'll make you cry and they'll make you admire the volunteers. All Hands illustrates that we can all find a way to give. Whether donating dollars or talent, we all can make a difference.

Carrie Morgridge
Vice president, Morgridge Family Foundation
and author of *Every Gift Matters*

Catching the "Wave"

My life changed course with a single sentence.

I've always been interested in the idea of a connected society. I have worked in the tech field for more than fifty years, where I am virtually connected to others through email and text messages. But it's face-to-face encounters with people that fascinate me, that define connection for me. It's of tremendous importance to me that I cultivate face-to-face relationships with colleagues and peers. That's how I found myself sharing lunch with Tim Tse, whom I'd met a year earlier when in Shanghai for a Tektronix board meeting.

Tim splits his time between Shanghai and Boston, so we agreed to get together when he was next in Boston—December 28, 2004. The earthquake that originated in Indonesia and the resulting tsunami that devastated communities across the Indian Ocean basin had occurred two days earlier. During our lunch, I made a casual remark that it was a terrible event. And that's when Tim responded with the words that literally changed my life.

"David," he said, "ten days ago, I was having lunch on the outdoor patio of the Meridien Hotel in Phuket, Thailand. Everyone who was on that patio two days ago was killed."

In that moment, a faraway event was brought much closer. After our lunch, I Googled "Meridien Hotel Phuket tsunami." I learned that Phuket, an island at the southwestern tip of Thailand poking out into the Andaman Sea, lies directly across the Strait of Malacca from the epicenter of the earthquake. It bore the brunt of the tsunami. Its popularity as a resort for tourists from around the world—and the fact that the tsunami occurred at the height of the holiday season—made it headline news around the globe.

The Meridien's website indicated that although two of its three hotels on Phuket were damaged and twenty-one people had been killed, one hotel remained open. Of note to me was the bullet on the side of the webpage that mentioned it still had high-speed Internet access. I began to consider how the Internet could be used to help from the middle of this massive disaster. In 2004, the Internet was still relatively new, but, thanks to my work in technology and later a boutique investment bank, I had a developed a considerable understanding of its capabilities.

The power of the Internet is connectivity: Getting the right information to the right people will generate the right result. Many disaster response organizations, trying to galvanize awareness and support for earthquake and tsunami victims, were still using a scattershot approach to engage the public, such as newspaper advertisements pairing photos of the devastation with general pleas for help. I was confident the Internet could offer another solution: presenting the specific needs of survivors to specific sources of relief. It's simply targeted marketing, a commonly used and highly successful concept in business. I suspected it could be effectively applied to disaster relief.

I began by calling the manager of the Meridien in Phuket. I soon learned a lesson that would be invaluable in subsequent interactions:

Managers of hotels in remote locations know how to get things done; they can access materials, they understand local employment practices, they interface with local government officials, they manage repair and construction, and they coordinate the logistics. The Meridien manager told me that the country was devastated but his hotel was fine, and he would be happy to support my efforts if I came to help. I'd never been to Thailand. In fact, I'd never been involved in anything remotely like this. The closest I had come to get-your-hands-dirty volunteer work was running a United Way campaign in Buffalo, New York. But, I had done a lot of "corporate-type" volunteering. I had served on two university boards and had been chair of the local cancer research institute, the Chamber of Commerce, and the IDA, so I had the desire to help and some knowledge of how to go about it.

As it happened, I was scheduled to attend a board meeting in Berlin on January 10. I figured that since I was traveling halfway to Thailand on someone else's dime, all I had to do was get from Berlin to Thailand. I had enough time to get organized and immunized, and I'd have a safe place to stay when I got there. The more I thought about it, the more I concluded, "Okay, maybe this isn't so crazy." I booked my airline tickets. I'd arrive in Phuket on January 21 and stay at the Meridien. I started pumping away on the Internet to learn more about disaster relief operations already at work in Phuket.

Among the many newspaper articles I read was one about the fishing village of Bang Tao, where a group of volunteers was making progress under the direction of an American named Mike Cegielski, who had been overseeing the construction of a budget hotel there (originally scheduled to open on January 1, 2005). It was in ruins as a result of the tsunami, but, as a result of his hotel operations responsibilities, Mike was the most connected person in Bang Tao. In passing, the article mentioned that Mike hailed from Springville, New York, a small town fifty miles south of my former hometown of Buffalo. I took it as a sign.

Tsunami strikes the village of Bang Tao, Thailand Dec. 26, 2004.

It was easy to track down an email address for Mike, with a unique last name like Cegielski, and I emailed him, "Could you use the help of another Buffalo Bills fan?" He replied right away, and that's all it took: I had a contact—and a bed—at the Meridien Royal Phuket Yacht Club, and a connection for a place to pitch in. I packed up everything I thought I should take to a major disaster zone, including wireless routers, six walkie-talkies, a digital camera, a laptop, a GSM phone, and a couple of rolls of duct tape (I had no idea how to use the duct tape). It turned out, though, that my most important assets couldn't be packed in a duffel bag.

My large network of friends in the technology industry, like so many people around the world, wanted to help. I thought, *I'll be able to be on the scene and find out what's really needed.* I sent out an email blast to my network: I would put $15,000 of my own money into a relief fund of sorts and, if anyone wanted to contribute, I'd spend it as if it were my own. I received $10,000 in donations on behalf of disaster victims.

I also brought decades of experience in business management. I was comfortable managing finances and cash flow. I knew how to leverage technology to make connections. And as a former CEO and board member for five corporations, I knew the international language of business and how to use it to collaborate with the people in charge. And, most importantly, I had a deep need to do something more than just write a check. I wanted to be directly engaged. I wanted more than the knowledge that I was making a difference; I wanted to *see* the difference being made.

I didn't realize it at the time, but I had stumbled on the key elements instrumental to the success of what would become All Hands Volunteers: a worthy cause, my own credibility, creative use of the Internet to make connections, and most of all, as I would soon discover, the immeasurable power of simply being there.

What's in a name?

All Hands Volunteers has had a few names in its ten-year history. Allow me to give you a brief snapshot of our names before we dive into the full story of what is now known as All Hands Volunteers.

Our initial project, in Thailand in January 2005, was simply called *The Bang Tao Recovery Project*. As we expanded our efforts to communities beyond Bang Tao, such as Surin and Kamala, we decided to change our name to something more broad and encompassing of our mission. We chose the name *HandsOn Thailand*, and used it from February to May of 2005.

Hurricane Katrina struck the Gulf Coast of the United States on August 29, 2005; in order to facilitate our response efforts, we decided to incorporate as a 501(c)(3) nonprofit organization. During the process of becoming incorporated, we chose to rename the organization HandsOn Worldwide, and we called our Katrina response project HandsOn USA. We used it from September 2005 to January 2006. However, due to the existence of a completely separate organization, called HandsOn Network, we chose a new working name—HandsOn Disaster Response—in February 2006. We explored working with Hands On Network, but eventually chose not to do so.

On August 31, 2010, we officially changed our name to All Hands Volunteers and adopted the blue hands logo, which has been a consistent brand since our early days.

CHAPTER 1

Being There

I could never have imagined that my first day in a disaster zone would include strapping on scuba gear and exploring one of the world's top diving destinations. There was concern that the tsunami had destroyed the coral reefs off Bang Tao, a significant tourist attraction for the village. Someone needed to find out how the reefs had fared, so I volunteered. We're all certified scuba divers in my family, so, for me, assessing the reefs for damage from the tsunami seemed worthwhile. That's where I intended to connect before I met Mike and the team at the Bang Tao base.

As it turned out, I didn't go diving. Once on base, I decided that I could make a bigger impact on land. I became Uncle Dave, the gray-haired advisor and go-between linking our sweaty, scruffy crew of volunteers and potential donors.

I decided to make Bang Tao my base, so I moved from the Meridien to the Laguna Phuket, a five-hotel complex managed by Andaman Resorts. The Laguna had high-speed Internet and, as part of their contribution to the tsunami relief effort, the resort management offered to let me stay at no cost. (This allowed me to add the money I would have paid for accommodations at the Meridien into my general donation pot.) Living in the hotel gave me access to a community of expatriates, as well as European and American tourists who had been vacationing in the area when the tsunami hit. Those connections dovetailed nicely with Mike Cegielski's local network that identified specific needs in the village.

Many of the local community's needs might never have made it onto the radar screen of large aid organizations, even though they were no less urgent and important. Take fishing boats, for example, which are necessary to Bang Tao's economy as a fishing village. The long-tailed fishing boats—big, heavy-hulled crafts with boat-length steering shafts that drive their propellers at one end and have four-cylinder automobile engines welded at the other—are sea-going vessels and expensive to build. The combination of hull, shaft, motor, and fishing nets totals $5,000 per boat; forty-three boats were destroyed in Bang Tao alone. Learning of the scope of the damage, I wondered, *What will happen to these people?*

Through the expat community, I met a British couple that had been sailing around the world when the tsunami struck. They were trying to identify ways to help. Ditto for a Dutch guy who had married a Thai woman and retired to Bang Tao. His wife spoke English and Thai and helped share the story of one fisherman and his family. The British couple communicated the fisherman's story to the Royal Thames Yacht Club, where they were members; the Dutch guy shared it with sailing friends in Amsterdam. Each community jump-started a series of cocktail parties—sailors *love* any excuse to drink and socialize—to raise the funds needed to begin replacing the fishing boats of Bang Tao.

Meanwhile, volunteers from all over the world were pouring into

Fisherman whose daughter was lost during the tsunami; he named his new boat after her.

Phuket. One of these volunteers, with exactly the right skills at the right time, ended up in Bang Tao. Darius Monsef, a whiz at designing and building websites, really wanted to take part in the physical labor of clearing and rebuilding the village. It quickly became obvious that he could make more of an impact sitting at a laptop. He and other volunteers handily built a website for the Bang Tao Recovery Project, complete with stories from villagers plus photographs. Thanks to Pete Kirkwood, an American working in a nearby village, we were able to link with a 501(c)(3) banking account to collect tax-deductible donations from people around the world. From Bang Tao, we expanded into several villages, and Pete suggested what became our new name: HandsOn Thailand. Our website proclaimed, "We're here helping!" HandsOn became a beacon for those who wanted to do something more than write a check, and they followed our beacon to Bang Tao.

SUV

I soon learned that SUV has an entirely different definition in the philanthropic community: spontaneous unaffiliated volunteer. HandsOn attracted SUVs who may not have been part of an official aid group, but were not really unaffiliated. Each person I met connected easily to person after person after person. Our little network was expanding exponentially as people heard about what we were doing and told *their* friends. By the end of my first week in Bang Tao, we had twenty volunteers on site, and we expected twenty more to arrive the following week. I thought, *If this were a venture-backed business, growing from twenty to forty people in a year, it would be considered high-growth. This is happening in one week!*

Luckily, I'd experienced challenging times in the growth of a company. I began my career at IBM but then joined a very small company and helped grow it to more than four thousand employees. I was aware that many risks might not work out, but some would. I believe that you shouldn't shy away from making a risky move, but you shouldn't put all of your assets against it either. If it fails, you've tried and you can still recover. For thirty-five years, decision-making in the face of uncertainty had been my job. Now, it seemed that my entire career had prepared me for this moment.

As HandsOn Thailand expanded in scope, we also expanded in credibility. Nonetheless, our real street cred derived from the simple fact that we were there. You can't establish trust with people you don't know over the phone or via email. You must do it face-to-face. And you must use a language they understand. I'm not talking about English or Thai or French or Dutch. I'm talking about corporate-speak and volunteer-speak. I was fluent in both.

Since I *was* a volunteer, and I had experience *being* there, I understood others' motivations. I identified with the willingness to do whatever seemed most useful in the moment. Flexibility like this is a consistent characteristic among our volunteers. Perhaps more significantly, my gray hair inspired trust both from enthusiastic but inexperienced volunteers looking for a little guidance and potential donors searching for a project aligned to their hearts and wallets. That's how we ended up forging a link between a tiny fishing village in Thailand and a high-end American ski resort in Utah.

When the managing director of the Stein Eriksen Lodge at Deer Valley, one of the most luxurious ski resorts in the US, raised tsunami relief funds from clients, friends, and neighbors in the Park City area, he contacted the Amanpuri, a super-lux peer resort in Phuket, to ask where to donate the funds. Because it was such a large sum—$60,000—he planned to travel to Thailand to evaluate their recommendation in person.

The Amanpuri folks had heard about HandsOn from their colleagues at Andaman Resorts and recommended our project to the lodge's director. Our guys had worked up a sleek PowerPoint presentation, printed some handouts, and organized a tour. The Stein Eriksen director saw an organization with a passionate and committed volunteer staff from all over the world and an American corporate style. He donated the entire $60,000 to us, knowing the money would be used effectively.

Big victories and innumerable smaller wins gave HandsOn the motivation to continue and the confidence that we were doing the right things the right way. Frankly, we could have been easily overwhelmed by a tsunami of despair. Often, it was easier to tackle the debris left behind by the waves than confront the shards of shattered lives—but sometimes you just couldn't avoid them.

Being There

One evening, a volunteer approached me. A Thai woman had come to her with a list of the things her few remaining family members needed, including a flashlight, hand puppets, and crayons. The woman had lost thirty-nine relatives in the tsunami. Imagining that poor woman's situation, I was overcome with a flood of emotions. I had to walk away because I didn't want to weep in front of this young volunteer, and I knew I was going to burst into tears. I grabbed the keys to our shared truck, hunted down a working ATM, withdrew $500 in Thai baht, and asked the volunteer to pass it on to the woman.

I'm normally an extremely pragmatic person with a very keen awareness of human reactions to money and power. But in Bang Tao, I found myself experiencing a wonderful suspension of cynicism. Every

A youngster finds reasons to smile despite injuries.

day, I focused on looking for the action that addressed a problem in the very real-world situation and then moved on to tackling the next problem. It was refreshing, but it was something much more, too. There was a sense of a secret being revealed—a secret breathtaking in its utter simplicity. When you show up to do good, people are motivated to help you. As Canadian clergyman Basil King famously said, "Go at it boldly, and you'll find unexpected forces closing round you and coming to your aid."

The way you prove your credibility is by being there. I cancelled my flight home twice before finally returning to Boston in mid-February. It was only three weeks after I had arrived in Thailand, but it seemed like a lifetime. The David who got off the plane at Logan Airport was a much different person than the one who landed in Phuket. From the beginning of my experience in Bang Tao, I'd accepted that our project was fundamentally transitional in nature. Our mission, as we eventually defined it, was to be on the ground providing immediate, essential support while larger organizations and the government prepared to bring their own capabilities to bear. But the commitment, effort, and pure compassion of our group and its supporters—some 323 people donated a total of more than $100,000 to our website—resonated for me long afterward, as powerful as it had been unexpected.

I wasn't the only one who felt that way. In June 2005, I received an email from Darius Monsef, the HandsOn website whiz. "That was the greatest thing I've ever done in my life," he wrote about our work in Bang Tao. "Can we do it again?' Two months later, Hurricane Katrina slammed into the Gulf Coast.

CHAPTER 2

From Bang Tao to Biloxi

I was planning to go to Darfur when Hurricane Katrina struck the Gulf Coast of the United States.

In June 2005, as the genocide and refugee crisis in Darfur, in western Sudan, was unfolding, Darius Monsef called and asked, "Could we do it again?" We'd only been back from Bang Tao for a few months.

We discussed what had drawn so many dedicated volunteers, and I opined that the tsunami was, at that time, the worst disaster in the world. We speculated the refugee crisis in Darfur might now warrant that superlative. Our experience in Thailand and the recognition for what we had achieved there gave me confidence that we could raise money for just about any crisis, as long as we could offer a real solution to a real problem. We started making plans.

Back in Boston, I met with Dr. Larry Ronan, a staff physician at Massachusetts General Hospital who also works with a global emergency medical response group. As we discussed Darfur, an idea came to me. There were about seventy nongovernmental organizations (NGOs) helping in Darfur, but travel in and out of the area was dangerous. What if we could operate a no-charge charter service from safe, nearby airports using Internet-based planning to fill empty seats? Darius and I planned to accompany Dr. Ronan when he visited Darfur in early November. Meanwhile, Dick Clinton, a burly cop from Tennessee and fellow Bang Tao alumnus, had been in touch and added himself to our Darfur group on the basis that he could "cover our backs."

Mother Nature Changes Our Plans

On August 29, 2005, Hurricane Katrina crashed into the Gulf Coast with winds of more than 125 miles per hour and a storm surge of over 25 feet. More than one million people in the region were displaced by the storm, which the Federal Emergency Management Agency (FEMA) later called, "the single most catastrophic natural disaster in US history." It is also the costliest hurricane in US history; FEMA's estimate for the total damage came to $108 *billion*.

Darius, Dick, and I decided Katrina would drown out any fundraising interest in our Darfur efforts. We tabled our trip to Sudan, committing to get to Darfur sometime in the future, and decided to respond to Katrina using the lessons we had learned in Thailand. We chose to take a three-pronged approach, based on our personal strengths and networks.

Dick started calling law enforcement contacts anywhere in the impacted area and eventually wangled an invitation from a Lieutenant he knew in the Gulfport, Mississippi, Police Department to stay in his home. This gave us access to their ad hoc emergency operations center,. Darius updated the HandsOnThailand website for a US response, including information for donors and volunteers. And I got us incorporated, applied for 501(c)(3) status, and set up checking accounts and an online donation portal. We officially launched on September 6, 2005.

One potential glitch arose: Darius wanted to jump in full-time but he had bills to cover. He had been a hero in Bang Tao, and I realized that our Katrina response had a better chance of succeeding if he could commit to being on-site full-time for the next few months. I agreed to pay him $1,000 a month. (Our compensation systems have evolved since then; we now pay key people a salary.) With the basic arrangements taken care of, we flew to Mississippi. We arrived in Gulfport, where we met Dick and some early volunteers, on September 7, 2005.

I think the reason All Hands has been successful is that David and I and the people who started it—we were all business entrepreneurs, and All Hands' success was about efficiency and scale. We cared about the people we were helping, but we came to it with a business mind. What I enjoyed was the logistics of it. I rarely got to clean someone's house and shake their hand and make the emotional connections. I was handling the logistics of twelve rental cars and forty college kids, and running the company from day to day. It just happened to be really meaningful work.

—Darius Monsef

HandsOn USA was ready to go. Now we just had to figure out how we could help and where we could be most useful. To many, *Katrina* was synonymous with New Orleans. New Orleans was in the news every day—and the devastation there was epic. Levees had failed. Eighty percent of the city had flooded. FEMA later calculated that seventy percent of New Orleans's housing was damaged, leaving hundreds of thousands of people homeless and in dire need of food, water, and shelter.

Frankly, I was intimidated by the news coming out of New Orleans. The scale of the destruction was just too big for HandsOn. I thought we should find a town that matched our capabilities, a Gulf Coast version of the Bang Tao village, where we could forge personal connections and make a difference. I'd learned in Thailand that a natural disaster isn't confined to one town—there's plenty of damage to go around. And while some places get major attention from the media and government and nongovernment organizations, some only get minimal support. Most, especially the smaller and/or less notable towns, get little to none.

Gulfport Seemed Like a Good Place to Start

Dick Clinton's connection to the local police department became invaluable. Authorities have a well-founded suspicion of outsiders who show up after disasters. Are they looters? Are they scam artists who promise aid in return for "just a small down payment," then pocket the money and disappear? However, we quickly overcame

The destruction across the Gulf Coast region was extreme.

suspicion because we were staying with a local policeman, and we were working with the police at their emergency ops center. We weren't viewed as strangers. And we were happy to show what we could do.

The police had been on twenty-four-hour duty since the hurricane hit, and they were stretched to their limit. They couldn't even take the time to address the needs of their own families. So, we started by helping the families of the on-duty police with their needs, like removing fallen trees and tarping roofs, among other things, and in the process gained their appreciation and trust.

We knew we couldn't make our host policeman's home the base of our operations. We needed a place that would be large enough to shelter and feed teams of volunteers, store our equipment, and park our vehicles. A hotel seemed like the appropriate venue, as it had been in Thailand. We were operating from what we knew, because we had used an affected hotel in Bang Tao. It had been under construction when the tsunami destroyed the first floor, including the lobby and offices, but the owner let us use the rooms on the second floor. But, when a Gulfport police family connection introduced us to representatives of the Beauvoir United Methodist Church in the neighboring town of Biloxi, we realized that this was not going to be the same as last time. The church became our home for the next five months.

....

Biloxi was the first time we got to figure out the systems of how we would do things. Bang Tao was just mixing all the chemicals and something good came of it. Biloxi was where we figured out which chemicals to mix and how to mix them.

—Darius Monsef

....

An officer from the Gulfport PD accompanied us to Biloxi, lending us credibility with the Biloxi Police Department, which, in turn, gave us credibility with Biloxi's mayor. We needed it—the National Guard was patrolling the streets demanding written proof that aid workers were legit. We typed up a letter that basically said, "We're with a real organization, not just two guys in a truck," and had the mayor sign it. We made stacks of copies, and carried one in each vehicle—an official "passport" of sorts. Darius designed bright-colored badges with bold print, laminated them, and strung them on lanyards for all of our volunteers to wear around their necks.

Like Bang Tao, Biloxi was big enough to absorb and provide for an influx of volunteers yet small enough that our contributions could make a significant difference. It was big enough that we could expand our operations, if necessary, but small enough that we could identify and respond to specific community needs. It was not too big, not too small but just right. In deciding to work in Biloxi, we learned to apply what we later called the *Goldilocks test*.

Biloxi was one of many Gulf Coast towns to suffer major damage.

Coincidentally, the day we saw the church and agreed to make it our base, I was interviewed by National Public Radio's Robin Young for her live news show, *Here and Now*. She described me as "an experienced disaster executive" on the basis of my work in Bang Tao. I was a bit taken aback by that description but, on reflection, realized it was accurate. HandsOn had the basics in place. We had a live website, 501(c)(3) status to accept donations (I had just received confirmation earlier that morning), and a base at 2113 Pass Road, Biloxi, Mississippi. Anyone who wanted to volunteer was welcome, I said on live radio. No financial contribution necessary, you just had to want to help.

It's remarkable how little things incrementally build on other little things until the puzzle pieces magically fall into place. Our website was in good shape. We had a physical address. The NPR endorsement allayed people's concerns. We sounded as though we knew what we were doing. And, in fact, we pretty much did. Our experience in Bang Tao enabled us to get up to speed quickly in Biloxi: We were there a little faster than other response groups, we were a little better organized, and we had a working model that let us adapt to local circumstances and kept us one step ahead. At the end of the radio interview, I invited listeners to come on down. They did.

Among those who responded were people who would become key to the success of the organization over the coming years, either as volunteers who metamorphosed into staffers or stalwart volunteers who showed up time and time again. Marc Young, Jeremey Horan, Bill Driscoll, and Stefanie Chang were each a key part of our Biloxi response, and each rose to key leadership roles with All Hands over the next several years. They were part of forming our culture and helping us stay grounded and connected to both the volunteers and the communities we served. Sue Glassnor is representative of what has become a powerful "alumni pool" of folks who are ready to answer the call whenever AHV announces a new project.

Jeremey Horan's experience is especially emblematic of many volunteers' initial experience with All Hands.

....

I donated money to the Red Cross and made some inquiries to Habitat for Humanity and the Salvation Army about actually volunteering, but I received "you have to take these classes, then you'll be put on an eligibility list" or "we're not responding at this time" emails, or I didn't hear anything at all. It was a very disheartening experience, because the news was telling the story of the devastation these families and communities were experiencing, and for the first time in my life, I felt overwhelmingly compelled to be involved.

Then, I read a blog by a guy traveling across the country who stumbled across the base camp in Biloxi. He basically said, "Here's a group of people doing incredible stuff. They'll take anybody and everybody who wants to do something."

The morning I learned about them, I went to their website and found that all you needed to do was tell them when you wanted to come and how long you wanted to stay for. I was working at an advertising agency in New York. I consolidated my remaining vacation days, booked a plane ticket, and set up a week-long trip to volunteer. My friends thought I was a little nuts. When I showed them the website, they said, "This doesn't seem real."

A volunteer came to the airport to pick me up. The only information I was given was that he'd be wearing a HandsOn USA T-shirt. He was a very dirty, older gentleman. We drove off to the base in Biloxi, this giant annex to a church, with sleep spaces on the floor and dozens of tents out back. A crowd of people was winding down for the day, but there was a positive energy to the place and I thought, "Let's do this." I got the rundown and hit the ground running the next day.

The week went by so incredibly fast. Two days before I was supposed to leave, I thought I had only scratched the surface of what I wanted to do. I emailed my boss to ask if I could stay for another week of unpaid leave. At the end of that week, the same feeling crept up: *I'm not really done, I want to stick around.* I sent another email to my boss. He said, "We can make it work, but if you're not back at work by next Monday, you don't have a job to come back to."

When I went back to New York, I spent the next six months thinking, "What am I doing here?" I had felt more productive, more connected, more fulfilled in the three weeks I spent in Biloxi than I had in three years of working for the agency. I thought, *I don't want to do this anymore.*

I gave notice in July 2006, just after my twenty-fifth birthday. Two days later, I flew to Indonesia to volunteer for the HandsOn earthquake relief project in Jogjakarta.

—Jeremey Horan

Within weeks of our arrival in Biloxi, our expected group of fifty volunteers had quadrupled to more than two hundred. We never looked back.

CHAPTER 3

Building Networks of Trust

When you bring a group of volunteers together, you never know what you'll encounter. The greatest challenge to an organization whose success depends on attracting committed volunteers is to make each and every individual feel that their contributions are productive and appreciated. Every now and then, an opportunity will crop up to highlight a special skill that you'd never dream would be applicable in the midst of a disaster (such as experience with photo retouching, which was a huge bonus in our later work in Japan). For the most part, you want volunteers who are putting in long hours of sweaty, smelly work day after day to feel not just productive but *exponentially* productive, whether they're building a school or mucking out a flooded house.

There's a delicate balance between what needs to be done and what volunteers want to do. Sure, there's a shared purpose to help the community. But what holds everything in balance—and what keeps volunteers coming back to do more—is trust between the organization and the volunteers. The organization carries on the conversations with community leaders, gathers local feedback, and chooses what tasks will be pursued. The volunteers must trust that those decisions are well made. In the case of HandsOn, both cohorts had to learn to trust each other. We had to learn how to reinforce the threads of trust between us in order to weave a robust and tight network we could all rely on, even when—especially when—the going got tough. It wasn't easy, as we learned in Bang Tao.

Mike Cegielski, who started what became HandsOn Thailand, had a military background; his training led him to expect people to do what he asked without his having to explain why or get buy-in. That became a problem. There was chatter in the volunteer community about his imperiousness, and some volunteers were even considering quitting. Volunteers—unaccustomed to a military way of giving and accepting orders—felt they had a right to know why we would focus on one issue versus another when there was so much need in so many different areas.

One night, I suggested that we try another way of getting buy-in from our volunteers. We hosted a one-hour happy hour for the volunteers followed by a Q and A session in which everyone could ask questions of me. It was a transitional moment—and it worked.

We shifted our operating paradigm to include transparency: Every volunteer had a right to know which tasks we were prioritizing and why. That became an intrinsic part of our operating model in Biloxi. Every evening, we would hold a meeting for everyone involved in the project. We placed a large white board front and center, listing the projects to be tackled the next day and the number of volunteers required for each one. Volunteers could select which task or team most appealed to them and how they wanted to participate. (A few years later, we updated this system to using a magnetic white board and having the volunteers put their name on magnets; they just shift the magnets instead scribbling their names.) The logistical and operational advantages to this system were easy to see: We'd always secure the correct number of volunteers for the task and every volunteer was aware of our projects. But the unexpected benefit was community building among the volunteers. People got to know each other better by swapping stories about their jobs, like ripping out muddy floorboards, or in shared tasks, like checking off supply deliveries. And we democratized the sign-ups by establishing the rule that anyone who signed up to wash dishes got first priority on the white board the next day. After volunteer sign-ups, we'd open the floor for questions and suggestions, further building a culture of transparency ✎ and community.

Some disaster response organizations have clearly delineated duties. For example, the Red Cross delivers hot meals. They arrive in a disaster area armed with the resources to drive through the area and deliver warm food—that's a major part of what they do. Although we have a basic mandate to offer physical labor to aid in cleanup efforts (clear debris, saw downed trees, tarp and de-mold broken buildings), we are proud to be flexible and responsive in the services we offer. There are many different paths back to normal life. That's why each disaster demands an open mind. We know that soon enough our blank slate will be covered with a to-do list of problems specific to each disaster, as well as creative solutions suggested by our volunteers.

....

We're like an emergency room doctor. We try to staunch bleeding and set broken bones and stitch up wounds so that people can get back on their feet. We focus on what we can do to get people started on the road back to living a normal life. We say, "We've learned all these random tricks along the way and we'll do whatever you want us to do." We're good at not doing things one way.

It's naïve to think you'll always know what you're doing. We've learned constantly, and that's all right with us. We're not dead set at how we do things. The only thing we've stuck to is immediate relief before normal life kicks back in.

—Darius Monsef

Envision a community in which a third of the buildings are destroyed or severely damaged and you'll have a sense of what Biloxi looked like in the wake of Hurricane Katrina. Landmarks and familiar places had been leveled, making it difficult for our volunteers to follow a local's directions. For example, residents would stop by our base at the church and say, "A tree crashed through our roof. We need help." We'd ask for their address and they'd respond, "You take a right where the McDonald's used to be." That's not helpful for people who don't know where the McDonald's used to be!

Here is Darius installing new street signs, each with our blue hand logo.

Darius came up with a straightforward solution: rebuild the street sign system. Laying out a city map, he identified the number of signs we'd need, purchased large plastic sheets and stick-on letters, and gathered volunteers to make new street signs. In my role of "adult supervisor," I suggested obtaining the mayor's approval, to be sure we had municipal buy-in for our efforts. With his approval granted, we set up a modified "quilting bee," in which volunteers cut the plastic sheets into strips and pasted on the letters for each street name. Darius had the inspired idea to add a blue HandsOn logo to each sign, subtly making our presence known and familiar. Volunteers nailed the signs to telephone poles, trees, or any other structure still standing near a street corner.

As the streets became identified as streets again, another problem emerged: Many locals had lost their cars. Volunteer Scott Erickson suggested we provide them with bicycles. I agreed to fund half the cost if he would kick in the other half; we committed $2,500 each, securing one hundred unassembled bikes. HandsOn volunteers put them together—complete with a blue HandsOn sticker—and the East Biloxi Recovery Center, an organization with which we worked closely, distributed them. Seeing these bikes on the street, allowing people to go about their daily business, was tangible evidence that we were meeting real and varied needs.

....

It was hard to comprehend true devastation until I saw a casino. The casinos were on these massive barges and by state law had to be surrounded by water. The storm had thrown the casino across the highway—a huge boat, five stories tall, cracked like an egg, with the innards of the casino spilling across the highway. You couldn't believe the force that caused that to happen.

You had the sense that people had lost everything, but they didn't look any different. I talked to a woman who had gone through the storm sitting in the rafters of her house, hoping the water wouldn't rise any higher. We all chipped in and bought her a mattress. She broke down crying. That's when I realized the depth of her loss: She'd been sleeping on the floor for the past three months.

—Adam Haber

....

During one of our nightly meetings, volunteer Helen Weatherall challenged us to look even more broadly at our mission. She mentioned that she had dropped in at the local SPCA on her way back to base in the afternoon, and they were overwhelmed and understaffed. So many Biloxians had evacuated that there wasn't enough staff to care for all the animals. Maybe we could help? Caring for animals seemed pretty far off our disaster response remit, but I posed the opportunity anyway. The assembled volunteers responded enthusiastically and our SPCA project task was born. We even built a kennel at our base, since volunteers would often rescue an animal that had reached the end of their "kennel life." When President Bush visited our base, two White House staffers took puppies back with them on Air Force One.

One of the most unusual but high impact volunteer proposals for assistance involved organizing and hosting the local high school homecoming dance. High school football is a big deal in Mississippi, and there's always a big dance to mark the beginning of football season. Since most of the students had lost their homes and clothes, the dance had been cancelled. A group of HandsOn women volunteers from Pennsylvania, whose children had already celebrated homecoming, proposed asking their kids and their friends to donate their party dresses. Volunteers on site would tailor them for the local girls.

When the dresses arrived in Biloxi, HandsOn volunteers organized a sewing circle to alter the clothing. Then, we put up a tent in the church parking lot, hired a local band, and gave the kids their big dance. We honored the local traditions through innovative problem solving.

....

We sent people out into the field who knew it was okay to find opportunities themselves or take whatever they were passionate about and see if they could help. At the nightly meeting, crews would report what they saw, or someone would say, "I ran into someone who was trying to rescue an abandoned dog from under a house. The Humane Society said they're really understaffed, and could we send them eight people." I might not have seen that opportunity about the pets, but someone else did.

At one point, we were staffing the Salvation Army warehouse, clearing rubble, cutting trees, helping the Humane Society, building a wheelchair ramp to the local synagogue, and repairing the roof on a Christian church. We had no agenda except the agenda to help however we could.

–Darius Monsef

While we gave our volunteers free rein, sometimes we had to rein them in. We learned that a volunteer organization must have rules, just like any company or workplace. We had expectations of our volunteers, and when they could not meet our expectations, we had the right to enforce the rules. For example, we expect volunteers to be ready to roll at 7:30 am. I remember one volunteer who said, "I'm a volunteer, and I want to sleep in until 10." My response was simply, "You can do that, but not here." He chose to leave rather than conform to our schedule. (We've followed that rule ever since, even if we're in Indonesia or the Philippines or places where it's not easy to be put out on the street.) Through the process of building our organization and managing volunteers, we have established a behavior code tailored to each locale and cultural climate that all volunteers must read and sign.

The biggest confrontation we experienced in Biloxi involved a chainsaw crew. The hurricane downed thousands of trees, damaging homes and blocking recovery efforts. From our initial chainsaw workers evolved a crew of about eight guys and a few women. "The Termites," as they dubbed themselves, were good at their work and proud of it. They began to acquire an elite status among the volunteers.

That's where the trouble began. Other volunteers wanted to join the crew but the Termites refused to include them. That led volunteers to ask, "What gives them the right to be the only ones who can handle a chainsaw?" As operations director, Darius tried to deal with the situation tactfully. The Termite leader pushed back and threatened to leave and take the rest of the gang with him. Darius told me he thought we could get our work done even if they walked, and we couldn't afford to be held up by any "special interest" group. I told him I trusted him. Darius ordered the Termites to accept others into their crew and, sure enough, they walked out. Darius recalled:

In any community, you naturally have leaders who self-establish and step up and take a role. That's great, but sometimes the direction they want to go is different. Because they're leaders and feel they're important, it's painful to cut their role. You think, *if they leave, this whole thing will fall apart.* But it finally comes to a head and you decide, okay, it's got to be done.

And, sure enough, other volunteers stepped up when the Termites left. It's the intrinsic nature of it—there's someone who would love to lead or has been watching from the sidelines and didn't step up because the role was already filled. If you believe the organism will fill the vacuum, it works out.

We learned a pragmatic lesson: Gaps will be filled.

No one volunteer is more valuable than another, but some volunteers *do* become integral to the running of the organization. Like Darius, Marc Young became one them. Marc had run dive boats all over the world, with a primary focus in Southeast Asia, earning him the nickname "Scuba." With his boat in dry dock storage for cyclone season, he found himself in Michigan visiting his mother when Hurricane Katrina hit the Gulf Coast.

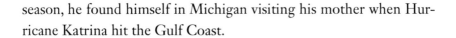

> I signed up for two weeks, but I had no idea how life-changing it would be. That happened to many people who volunteered who were looking for a different purpose to their life, but I was actually making money in the scuba-diving industry and living in paradise. I gave that up to chase disasters.
>
> **—Marc Young**

Having been turned away from volunteering with the larger organizations, Marc took it upon himself to travel to Biloxi, chainsaw in hand, to pitch in. He heard about HandsOn while driving south, and joined us on September 8, 2005. He recalled, "I started off cutting trees, but soon my management experience and life experience put me into overseeing a crew of people. Then, I started helping Darius with the management of the project. There was no ownership, just a sense of, 'Wow, we've got this huge task. How can we handle it?'"

By November, we had more than 150 volunteers at our base. Marc had business experience, management experience, and expertise in being responsible for the safety of others. We hired him as our second operations director on December 1, 2005. He stayed with HandsOn for the next seven years.

Marc recalled, "When David offered me a job at $800 a month and I said yes, his response was, 'Really?' He was so surprised I would give up what I was doing to be in a disaster zone. But it was actually a pretty easy decision. I'd had an amazing lifestyle. I was living in a version of some people's paradise. I was diving every day, which I love. I got pretty self-centered." He continued:

Fast-forward to this culture of giving, of helping people who need help, the immediate satisfaction that comes from each day being able to see the progress, even if it's just cleaning out an irrigation canal or gutting one house. Every day, you see what your effort has helped accomplish. That's addicting. And if you're part of a huge bureaucracy where it's a three- or seven-year slog to get to a goal, and, instead, you start out the day with the goal of mucking out a basement and at the end of the day the basement is mucked out, that's a huge accomplishment. That's addicting, too.

Our three-person management team spent time contemplating "what's next?" Since Darius and I had first worked together in Thailand, and Marc had worked in the scuba diving business outside the US for the past seven years, we were all aware of the international needs for disaster response. It led us to conclude that we could be most effective if we could apply our newly gained expertise wherever the need arose. My research found that 75 percent of people affected by natural disasters were located within the Ring of Fire, the area of southeast Asia bordering the Pacific Ocean that includes island nations like Indonesia and the Philippines. This area would become the focus of the next projects for our new organization.

By the end of 2005, I'd realized that HandsOn must start seriously planning for the future. I'd thought of Bang Tao as a once-in-a-lifetime event for me. Hurricane Katrina presented an opportunity to start a sustainable organization. Instead of the life I'd envisioned as a retired CEO—serving on corporate boards, investing in start-up companies, spending more time with my family—I was about to enter the disaster response business.

CHAPTER 4

Growing Pains

The title of The Clash song, *Should I Stay or Should I Go?*, pretty much encapsulate the sentiments felt by a disaster relief organization working in a disaster zone at a certain point in the recovery process.

As a community hauls itself back to its feet after a major natural disaster, its relationship with volunteer responders goes through what is now a predictable cycle: First, the community thanks you for all of the work you're doing; next, it wonders whether you're licensed to do that work; then, it asks, "Why are you taking our jobs?"

There's a brief window of time during which the rules around licensing and other work-related restrictions are suspended. For example, in the early weeks after a disaster, volunteer nurses are eagerly welcomed to provide first-aid care; but, after a few months, the state will stop looking the other way regarding labor laws. As the community regains some sense of normalcy, the rules gradually come back into effect. It's a natural progression to which the relief organization must be sensitive, reading the signals coming from the community so that it does not overstay its welcome.

Based on our experience in Bang Tao, I decided that three months was the appropriate period of time to stay in Biloxi. We arrived on September 6, so our mission announcement stated that we'd be there until December 6. Weeks later, we recognized that we had become so integral to the community's recovery from so much trauma and change, it was unthinkable for us to pack up and leave two weeks before the holidays. We announced that we would remain in Biloxi until January 16. After that, I figured, I'd return to my regular routine.

But, in November 2005, I received a letter that changed everything. It turned out that another aid group with the words HandsOn in their name already existed. HandsOn Network was not happy that HandsOn Worldwide, the name under which we'd incorporated, and HandsOn USA, the project name for our operations in Biloxi, shared a moniker. They notified us that we were infringing on their trademark. It could have been a disaster for us. Instead, it provided a solution to problems both organizations were experiencing.

HandsOn Network had been in business for some twenty years. They were a solid organization and solidly funded. At HandsOn Worldwide, in contrast, we were constantly scrabbling for money, our bank account as bare as the buildings we stripped. If we could somehow come to an understanding, I reasoned, HandsOn Network might be the path to lead us to the corporate financial support we so desperately needed.

HandsOn Network and HandsOn Worldwide negotiated a buyout, as it would have been called in the corporate world. HandsOn Network took over our Biloxi base on January 31, 2006: They absorbed our volunteers, moved our existing long-term volunteers into paid staff positions, and took possession of our on-site equipment. That gave them what they really wanted: HandsOn Gulf Coast, a solid platform in the region.

In return, they provided us with $150,000 in cash and proclaimed themselves satisfied when we changed our name to HandsOn Disaster Response (HODR), on the basis of the understanding that we'd transition into their disaster response unit. That gave us what we wanted: the funds to keep going for at least another year. On February 1, 2006, the deal was finalized. I was executive director of HODR, and I was officially in the disaster response business.

The HandsOn Network deal afforded us the financial ability to retain Darius and Marc—a critical element of our survival as an effective organization. With HandsOn Network's financial support, I could increase Darius's and Marc's compensation from $1,000 a month to an annual salary of $40,000, the approximate amount they would have received if they had transferred to HandsOn Network. That allowed HODR to commit to these guys for a year, and for them to commit to us. Additionally, having experienced disaster managers on staff also allowed me to continue my work serving on corporate boards in addition to my unpaid commitment to HODR.

After we concluded our work in Biloxi in early 2006, Darius and Marc went on a trip around the world, stopping in potential hot spots for natural disasters—think San Francisco and Thailand—to meet with local officials. My corporate background had taught me the usefulness of building personal relationships with people you might someday want access to in order to allow you to reignite your connection when needed. So, Darius and Marc traveled the globe to share our story and encourage localities to share their disaster preparedness plans. Together, we forged relationships. Officials in disaster-prone areas were made aware of us. When disaster struck, we felt they would take our call.

In our relationship-building travels, we learned useful lessons about offering aid in developing countries. As Darius recalled, "When

Marc and I went to Banda Aceh in Indonesia [the major city closest to the epicenter of the 2004 earthquake, which suffered massive damage from both the earthquake and the resulting tsunami], we began to see how NGOs work together—or don't." Darius and Marc had observed the competitive nature of NGOs and how some took a scarcity approach to their work. Some NGOs would hoard whom they wanted to help and how they would allocate their resources, rather than sharing and collaborating.

In one example, a German NGO working in Indonesia built houses with kitchens, while a Dutch group built houses without kitchens but with bathrooms. Darius observed, "We learned that when we go to third-world places, we want to leave them better off, but we should focus on understanding their culture and their way of doing things and not impose or force our culture on their community." We also learned the limits of our efforts in regard to where and in what kind of disaster we can help. "We went to Kabul in Afghanistan," Darius explained, "and concluded that we will not do projects in war zones. It's just too dangerous."

It's always a joy to interact with the kids – just ask Suzie Lee!

Thankfully, 2006 did not present HandsOn with any Katrina-sized cataclysms that year, but Mother Nature dished out plenty of misery for impoverished people who lacked the resources to protect themselves. In June, we launched Project Jogjakarta in Indonesia on a four-month debris-removal and rebuilding effort in the village of Sawit on the island of Java.

It was on that project that April Jelinek joined us. She recalled,

> While I was home from India for Christmas, the visa laws changed and I had to wait three months before I could return to India. All Hands (then HODR) had a project in Indonesia, so I sent them an email. I didn't think anything would come of it, but two hours later, I had an email from Tom Taylor saying, "Yes, of course, we'd love to have you. Buy a plane ticket, send us dates, and we'll pick you up at the airport." Having someone pick me up at the airport—now that was service!

The Sawit project was a small one, with only about thirty volunteers helping local families clear debris, salvage building materials, and clean up home sites. The volunteers became like family, and we bonded deeply with the community.

One experience stands out for April, and encapsulates for her what it meant to work for HandsOn:

> When we arrived on the first day, the mom, dad, grandmother, aunt and uncle from down the road, three or four kids, and families of neighbors were all assembled and ready to help. The grandmother was about eighty years old, but she sat there and cleaned bricks all day. After three days, we

hadn't quite finished. The family came to our base in tears, saying, "Please, we can't finish on our own."

We were scheduled to work elsewhere, but we really wanted to help this family. By that time, our salvage team was so well coordinated that we didn't even need to talk. We just knew what we needed to do. We finished early on the other site and came back to this family. When the mom saw our truck pull in, she just started crying. We finished the whole site.

That was when I decided, I had to stay with this organization.

....

As April's experience illustrates, HandsOn has never lacked for volunteer commitment, but the shot in the arm that we expected from the HandsOn Network deal was beginning to look less and less like a reality for us. Typhoon Reming hit the Philippines in the Fall of 2006, and since HON (Hands on Network) had an affiliate in Manila, this seemed like a perfect chance to work together. But HON had encountered some economic challenges of their own, and CEO Michelle Nivens told me they couldn't offer us any financial support.

By the end of 2006, we realized that our anticipated partnership with HandsOn Network wasn't happening—nor was the funding we expected from them materializing. As we moved into 2007, once again we were running short of cash. We reduced our expenses when Darius left to start his own business. Marc and I were determined to keep going. We had completed two successful projects in 2006, and although they had exhausted most of our funds, we had gained a year's experience in widely varied locations. We knew we could be effective in any situation—if we could just raise enough money.

We worked in the Philippines through April, 2007, tarping roofs, repairing schools, even planting coconut trees. We established great relationships with the local community and leadership. We raised enough money to cover our modest expenses, and gave everyone a post-project break. Then a major earthquake hit Pisco, Peru, on August 15, 2007, and we decided to answer the call.

(top left) Future barangay captain Noel Estilomo and Scuba Marc planning in San Isidro, Philippines. (top right) Enthusiastic E building 'her school' in Pisco, Peru. (bottom left) Many hands make light work. (bottom right) Flower on the newly renovated school wall made by girls' handprints.

Hosting more than five hundred volunteers over the course of the project, it was the organization's largest international deployment and largest reconstruction project to date. Lee Keet, one of my colleagues in the CEO Roundtable, joined HandsOn on the project. Lee recalled, "I was assigned to work on constructing a school . . . I designed and built the bathroom for these kids. We didn't have any power tools, so it was all built by hand. Nancy [Lee's wife] dug post-holes with a trowel. We found a cement mixer, but we had no fuel for the motor; it took four people about an hour to mix one batch of concrete. We didn't have rebar, so we scavenged rebar from the downed school and bent it back into shape. We rebuilt everything but the roof." HandsOn had certainly learned how to improvise and be resourceful. What surprised Lee even more was HandsOn's "willingness to do just about anything."

Project Pisco was in the process of being wrapped up because the area had become unsafe. Pisco is like the Marseilles of South America, only more violent. Some volunteers had been robbed at knifepoint. With a volunteer group from Burning Man coming in to help, I turned the project over to them. But Lee was troubled that he had not been able to build the school's roof. As we were en route from Pisco to Lima, he told me, "The one thing I know is that if we don't tie the building together properly, the kids are going to be in school when the next earthquake hits and will die. We've got upright walls with rebar sticking out. All we need to do is put on the roof."

I responded, "But we're already out of Pisco." Lee countered, "E could do it if she had money and supplies." E was a young Irishwoman who had become an integral part of our team and had stayed behind to continue working on the project. Lee and I decided we would pool our money for E to use to purchase roofing supplies. She drove from Pisco to Lima to meet us and pick up $2,500 in blank traveler's checks. It was a dangerous trip between Lima and Pisco, especially for a woman traveling alone, but she got back safely, secured the supplies, and she and the volunteers got the roof on the school.

Lee observes, "David's willingness to do just about anything so impressed me that at that point, I figured if he wanted to build up this organization, I might as well become a major donor. That's when I made the challenge grant that allowed him a safety net. It's really an endowment, but it can be invaded for emergencies." Lee's grant provided a much-needed shot of financial support that helped to keep HandsOn moving forward in its mission.

Even before Project Pisco was completed, Cyclone Sidr lashed the Bay of Bengal, devastating one of the most remote areas of Bangladesh and causing us to initiate Project Rayenda. Ian D'Arcy recalled,

Rachel led our project replacing 21 destroyed fishing boats. Philippines, 2006.

Shy students in Bangladesh giggle with a volunteer who visits their makeshift classroom.

"Bangladesh was one of my favorite projects. I was traveling from the capital of Dhaka by paddlewheel steamboat up the Buriganga River to get to the project. When I told a young English couple where I was going, they asked, 'Can we come, too?'" The couple stayed on the project for six weeks—longer than Ian himself—and became an integral part of the project simply by chance of meeting Ian on the boat. That's testament to the power of the HandsOn mission.

The Bangladesh project site was very remote. Because there were no other NGOs in Rayenda and only thirty HandsOn volunteers, we shared a sense of being isolated in the community. With materials provided by Save the Children, we helped build a school and playgrounds. Ian sums it up: "It was a very intimate, very moving experience."

For the first time, HandsOn found itself running two projects simultaneously, on opposite sides of the globe. That was a big decision for our little organization. The fact that we could pull it off is testament to the dedication of a worldwide volunteer base that was eager and willing to help. Our projects in Peru and Bangladesh were turning points in another way, too, as Marc Young remembered. At a meeting with the mayor of a small town in Peru, he was forced to adjust his perspective on HandsOn's building efforts.

....

I had always advocated against building shelters because there was no way we could ever meet all the needs and I didn't want to play God and decide who got a shelter and who didn't. But when the mayor of a small town in rural Peru gave me a beautiful PowerPoint presentation about the need for shelters in his community, it just blew me away.

At the end of it, I said, "Mr. Mayor, that was an amazing presentation. But I'm here to talk about irrigation canals, not houses." He said, "We can talk about irrigation canals, but this is the greatest need for my community: shelter." I said,

"You need twenty thousand shelters and we don't have the budget." And he replied, "But Marc, if you built two shelters, that would be two less than we need, and those families would be so happy."

That conversation changed my opinion and the All Hands approach. We realized we couldn't address the entire community but why shouldn't we help the people we can help? If there's a need, why wouldn't you address the portion of it that you can address? We decided, we'd do whatever we could.

....

We carried that lesson to Bangladesh, where we approached village elders and said, "We can only build twelve houses." The village elders determined who was most in need, so we didn't have to play God. We designed and built houses in a program we called the "HODR half": We would build half of the structure, and the people who would be living in it would build the other half. Marc observes, "That was a big turning point for me and a huge turning point for All Hands, which is now in the shelter business."

Our successes were tremendous. Our financial resources were another matter. HandsOn Disaster Response had built its reputation over the past two years in international aid. But in order to continue our work—and continue to expand—we needed stronger, more reliable funding. We realized that we had to operate where the greatest number of donation dollars is: the United States. That meant radically changing the scope of our operations and our business model. It meant running what were, essentially, two very different

Matriarch of an extended Bangladeshi family shows a volunteer how to efficiently use a machete.

businesses—one domestic and one international. And it meant convincing more people that what we had done was worthwhile and that we would—and, with their help, could—continue doing it.

CHAPTER 5

Coming of Age

I will never forget November 4, 2005. It was my birthday, and I was preoccupied about HandsOn's finances. We were still actively working on the Biloxi project, but we only had enough cash to cover ten more days of operations. When Eric, my partner in an investment banking business, called to wish me happy birthday, I broke down in tears.

"We're doing such good work, but we're running out of money," I choked out. "If we had time to tell people about our work, they'd send us money, but we're running out of time, too."

Eric knew me well and knew the depth of my commitment to HandsOn. Without hesitation, he said, "We'll wire you $25,000."

It was one of the best birthday presents I've ever received, and it enabled HandsOn to keep going.

Eric's donation is unique in the financial landscape. Donors don't give because an organization is desperate. When running a business, cash flow problems are effectively addressed by selling goods or assets and raising revenue. But you can't make a sales pitch by saying, "If you don't give me money, I'll go out of business." Similarly, with fund-raising, it's not, as the saying goes, a high-yield strategy. Just as in a commercial business, you can't use the "we're almost out of business" as a long-term growth plan. So, too, with fund-raising for a nonprofit: People want to believe they're supporting a healthy operation that will stay in business.

As the founder of HandsOn, I constantly asked myself, "How far into my own pockets should I reach? Were we failing if we couldn't raise money from other sources?" I didn't mind being the just-in-case fund in those early years, but it was not a sustainable or permanent financial solution.

HandsOn needed to buy time—literally. I calculated that we required $250,000 a year in stable, predictable, non-project-related funds for the next two years to build a stronger capability. We could not achieve that solely through the kind of spontaneous contributions that had supported our Biloxi operations and, to a large extent, our subsequent international work.

We quickly realized that we must make the strategic decision to add a domestic disaster response capability, so that US donors could see our efforts more clearly. We realized that current and potential US donors, for the most part, would be less interested in donating to cyclone relief in Bangladesh or earthquake recovery in Peru—especially if the natural disasters themselves failed to make front-page headlines—than they would be to donate to a crisis in their own backyard. Achieving successful results in our projects in Bangladesh and Peru reinforced our confidence that we could be successful in Missouri or Iowa. The domestic disasters might not seem as logistically challenging but responding to domestic events resonates with domestic donors. And in this business—and I came to believe HandsOn must be run like a business—you must be sensitive to your funding sources, especially the sources I had in mind.

Once again, I reached out to my friends. I asked fourteen friends to commit to give $25,000 annually for two years. It was a huge ask—we'd never received an individual donation of that size before—and a hugely personal one. Nine friends—we called them the Super Friends—responded to my call. They joined me, and together we gave enough to keep us in business. (We'll talk more about fundraising, and donors will explain why they support All Hands in chapter 10.)

One of the first goals we met with our operating fund was to hire Bill Driscoll. After his time with HandsOn in Biloxi, Bill had remained in Mississippi to start his own small organization to continue the work of rebuilding. As HandsOn was acquiring international experience, Bill was developing deep domestic expertise. He was the natural choice to become our director for domestic operations.

During 2008, HandsOn built what has become a domestic capability as strong as our international work. While there may be a fair amount of overlap, we learned that the domestic response model often calls on different donors, different partnerships, different volunteers, and different approaches to volunteer management. The fact is, there's a set of people who would never travel to Bangladesh but who are eager and willing to spend a week or two clearing tornado debris in Arkansas: students on spring break, school and church groups that hire a van and drive to our site, families who switch their vacation plans. Local residents are another huge pool of volunteers, since they can see firsthand how their neighbors are impacted. And because local volunteers live nearby, housing isn't the issue it is in, say, the Philippines. In our project in Cedar Rapids, we had to secure housing for 500 volunteers but an additional 1,500 could return to their own homes after a day's work. Local companies, too, become a rich source of volunteers and financial support.

We honed our skills early in 2008 in "Small D" disasters by focusing on short (i.e., no longer than one month) responses to tornadoes in Arkansas and Missouri. In comparison, we'd never stay for *less* than three months to aid in an international event.

On June 13, 2008, after weeks of rain, Iowa's Cedar River crested to more than thirty-one feet, its highest level in history, flooding ten square miles of the city of Cedar Rapids and displacing more than ten thousand residents. We were there a week later.

Project Cedar Rapids was a Big D domestic. Bill Driscoll described one of the major challenges for HandsOn. "The city initially decided to keep out any aid agencies that were not government, and the city was hesitant to start the cleanup effort because of concerns about liability. So, we relocated to Palo, a town of six hundred houses, almost all of which were flooded. We were able to funnel volunteers to the area and get results and build trust there very quickly. By proving ourselves in Palo and establishing our credibility, when the climate opened up in Cedar Rapids, we were right there. We stayed four months."

In Cedar Rapids, we had to respond differently in terms of the scale of fund-raising. A breakthrough came in the form of Adam and Renee Haber, a Long Island couple who had donated money to our project in Biloxi (Adam had been a volunteer there, as well) and came to Iowa with their two kids to volunteer. Renee remembered,

My husband and I had considered making a financial donation. We thought maybe we could use it to persuade other people to donate, too. I'm on the board of my local Jewish Community Center, and I understood the concept of getting the local community involved, so I asked, "Who are the big businesses? Who can we call?"

Adam came up with the idea of contacting the chamber of commerce and the mayor. We researched large family foundations on our cell phones and from a landline in an office. Our message was, "My husband and I are here from

Long Island. We're here because we care about your community but we can't believe that we care more than you do. We're willing to put up $50,000 if you'll match it before we leave. We want to meet you in person to discuss it before we go back to New York in two days."

....

Adam's idea was inspired, but after nearly two days of no response, he began to wonder about its impact. "We made a host of calls and the mayor made a bunch of calls but we didn't seem to get anywhere," he said. Just as the Habers were about to head to the airport, the CEO of Aegon, a major insurance corporation headquartered in Cedar Rapids and the largest corporation in the area, returned his call. The CEO agreed to send his representative to meet Adam and Renee for a last minute, pre-departure lunch.

Aegon already had in place a community service policy through which their employees would donate their time for one workday per month. Adam thought they'd want to give more. Marc Young recalled, "Adam's ballsy move was to call up Aegon and say, 'You have a foundation. Where does the rubber hit the road?' He had done the groundwork via phone and he basically said, 'You can double your money but I'll put it up only if you'll put it up.' The Aegon rep replied, 'Okay. You can pick up the check at three this afternoon.'" Marc continued, "We had one of those 'Holy shit, that just happened!' moments. Remembering it still gives me goose bumps." In response to our proposal, Aegon set up the Aegon USA Charitable Foundation specifically to aid us. It triggered an outpouring from other community sponsors. "We were hoping to get $50,000 for our $50,000. As it turned out, we raised $150,000 on top of the $50,000 we gave," Adam recalled. Our largest local donation to date had been in the range of $10,000. Adam and Renee Haber's efforts opened doors for us, not only in funding but also in other surprising ways.

After volunteering with us in Iowa for one week, Andrew Kerr quit his banking job to volunteer full-time for the duration of the project. When he became aware of our struggles to raise money, he said, "I can help." Having him smile and dial—chasing down funding leads at corporations, local foundations, and national charitable organizations—took a huge load off me. As he tells it, he couldn't stay away from HandsOn. Having returned with a family friend for a second stint on the Cedar Rapids project, he "noticed that as more volunteers arrived, the project was short on administrative staff. I realized I didn't want to go home, so I asked Bill Driscoll if it were possible to stay longer. He said, 'Yeah, that sounds great.' So, I drove back to North Carolina, dropped off my family friend, came back to Iowa, and stayed with HandsOn for another four years." Andrew became HandsOn's first director of development.

He never imagined that he would apply his banking expertise in such a way. "My role evolved first to leading teams of other volunteers, then coordinating the project with Bill and Jeremey Horan," he remembers. "Because I had been working in loan banking when I first signed on, I worked with people to qualify them for rebuilding grants. It was a skill set I didn't think would ever apply in a disaster zone. I was making good money in banking, but I had lost the happiness of the job. With All Hands, there's a great sense of purpose." We quickly agreed that the best way Andrew could contribute was in fund-raising, and he had a great impact there.

At the close of 2008, we also decided to expand our board of directors, adding two new director positions as part of our commitment to secure the growth and permanence of the organization. My approach to filling the board seats was to seek people who had volunteered with us, who understood firsthand the impact of what we did, as well as who had additional relevant experiences and abilities to complement those already on the board. This strategy worked so well that we've followed it ever since.

Although our expanding domestic operations were in the spotlight, we hadn't neglected international projects. One that would resonate with unexpected repercussions for years was Project Gonaives in Haiti. In less than four weeks, between August and September 2008, four fierce tropical storms and hurricanes hammered northern Haiti, saturating the country's deforested mountains and triggering landslides that coated the city of Gonaives in mud three feet deep. We launched our Project Gonaives on October 10, and stayed until the end of March, 2009. More than 150 volunteers from 14 countries joined us.

All Hands Volunteers procures the tools necessary to allow our volunteers to be effective.

Project Gonaives was our fifth international project, so we were becoming known in the BINGO (Big International NGO) community: We had formed relationships with organizations such as UNICEF, United Nations OCHA (Office for the Coordination of Humanitarian Affairs), Oxfam, Save the Children, and others. We quickly realized that coming to the table with a pool of willing volunteers makes you an attractive partner to such organizations. For example, UNICEF received a donation of one thousand daypacks and an equally large shipment of school supplies, but the organization lacked a storage facility for them and the bodies to unpack them. HandsOn provided the volunteer labor for that essential last mile of the delivery process, setting up an assembly line to break down the bulk boxes, fill each daypack with yellow pads and pencils, and present them to local schools. Marc Young observed, "We knew we had an asset for other organizations that had money but didn't have human resources on the ground. We had the ability to do stuff. Everyone else had money but had challenges implementing. We were implementers."

Gonaives was also our first experience organizing a local volunteer program. Young Haitian men often hung around our base, some out of curiosity and some hoping for paid work. In response, our staff started a work/career guidance initiative. We taught them basic job skills (like the importance of arriving at work on time), offered training in English, and helped write resumes they could use to apply for jobs with other NGOs.

Stefanie Chang emerged as a natural leader during her time with Project Gonaives. Until Haiti, she'd worked on multiple international projects but had never been in charge of one. She became a clear leadership choice for HandsOn due to her fluent French and three years of experience with our organization. It was irrelevant that she was only twenty-six years old. As I'd seen with Darius Monsef, age doesn't matter when managing disaster response. Success comes down to getting the job done, and Stef did it brilliantly.

We were worried about going into Haiti. Would it be safe? Could we be effective? As it turned out, it *was* safe and we *were* effective. "Going into Haiti," Andrew Kerr summed it up, "there was apprehension. You hear that Haiti is a very violent place and, in the movies, Haitians are all drug dealers and gangsters. But, while it was a rough situation, working with HODR you had a roof over your head, worked with people who made sure you got to the job site safely, had the right tools, and were fed."

By the end of 2009, we were feeling pretty confident in our organization. Thanks to the Super Friends, we had built a solid foundation for domestic operations that, in turn, raised our profile for international fund-raising. We had hired and maintained a core staff that was not only committed but also experienced in the areas we needed our organization to continue to grow. We'd made solid connections with other aid organizations. We'd proved we could be effective in five countries, including Bangladesh and Haiti, where widespread misery made them bywords for foreign aid sinkholes.

In 2010, our reputation and our confidence would be tested in ways we could never have imagined.

CHAPTER 6

"Our first five years prepared us for Haiti. Haiti will prepare us for the next five years."

In the late afternoon of Tuesday, January 12, 2010, a devastating 7.0 earthquake shattered Haiti, claiming the lives of more than 230,000 people. The earthquake destroyed homes and schools throughout the country and catalyzed Project Léogane, HandsOn's largest, longest, and most extensive international project to date. The Haiti earthquake was a *really* Big D—the most significant natural disaster since Hurricane Katrina. When it occurred, we were in the middle of an earthquake response project in Indonesia. We had seen the damage earthquakes could do, and we knew the situation in Haiti would be magnitudes worse. Just thinking about it made my stomach clench.

But we had already done a project in Haiti, so I knew we *could* do a project in Haiti. My first call was to Marc Young, our international operations director, then working on Project Sungai Geringging in Indonesia, to pack up and head to Haiti. To my surprise, about four hours later, I received a thoughtful—and thought-provoking—email from Stefanie Chang, Project Sungai Geringging director. She tactfully but firmly explained that it would be more effective to appoint *her*

AHV hosts a farewell party for our new friends in Sungai Geringging, Indonesia.

as the project director in Haiti: She had run our earlier Haiti project in Gonaives, she had maintained local contacts, and she spoke French. She was absolutely right, and I was embarrassed that I hadn't thought of it. Marc stayed in Indonesia and Stef flew to Florida to meet me.

Barry Goldsmith, a Gonaives volunteer and a generous supporter, offered us his home in Ocean Reef, a gated community on Key Largo with its own airstrip, as our launchpad as we figured out our next moves. Stef and Jeremey Horan, another experienced project director, flew in, and we began strategizing how to send in an assessment team. Stef recalled, "Other [disaster relief] organizations usually have an established presence in a country beforehand. We don't. So, we did what we do at beginning of any project: We contacted anyone we knew who might know someone in that place. We call it *casting the net*. It always serendipitously works out." In Haiti, as in other project launches, we found locals who were not only useful but generous with their time and local knowledge—people who were trustworthy and could be advocates to help connect us with the right people. We knew how to make inroads into the international

NGO community but found it more challenging and more important to build a productive relationship with the local communities. As an added benefit, Stef said, "It's fun to see the local people getting hired."

While we were reconnecting with our network in Haiti, Barry shared our mission with the community of Ocean Reef. I was invited to speak at two church services on Sunday morning. Almost every staff member in the Ocean Reef community is Haitian; anxious about their friends and loved ones, the whole community was eager to support us. Max Sanon, the senior manager of the mostly Haitian Ocean Reef staff, joined our team. Max is not only fluent in Creole but he also had a house outside of the capital of Port-au-Prince, where we could stay while we looked for a project site. With our connection to Max and to Barry, we became Ocean Reef's trusted vehicle to help Haiti; the community ultimately raised more than $100,000 to support our efforts, in addition to providing us with other resources.

An Ocean Reef resident with a plane flew us to the Dominican Republic (the airports in Haiti were restricted); from there, we drove to Port-au-Prince. Port-au-Prince was absolute, unimaginable chaos—the worst I'd ever seen. It wasn't a place for our group. Like New Orleans after Katrina, it was receiving all sorts of attention while other places weren't even a blip on the radar screen.

We headed west toward the epicenter of the earthquake in an SUV secured by Max. Twenty miles—and two hours later—we finally arrived in Léogane. To us, navigating the wrecked roads and anarchic traffic, it seemed far removed from Port-au-Prince, but it was close enough geographically that volunteers could fly into the Port-au-Prince airport when it resumed operations. Léogane was like a Haitian version of Biloxi: At 200,000 residents, it was big enough to support an All Hands project and small enough that we could make a difference.

Project Léogane officially launched on February 15, 2010, after we had secured buy-in from the town mayor. Stef had been in touch with her contacts in Gonaives, including people who had worked on our project and young men who had participated in our job training program. They helped us get established in Léogane while we put out a call for volunteers.

Port-au-Prince looked as if an atom bomb had gone off in the middle of the city. Léogane was almost 80 percent destroyed.

—Jack Ferrebee

Earthquake cleanup is basic and brutal: You break up debris into manageable-sized pieces, shovel it out of the way, and haul it off, wheelbarrow by wheelbarrow. Sometimes you find bodies. In the center city, cleanup is often focused on the massive piles of debris left in the wake of large building collapses. We felt we could have more immediate impact by focusing our efforts on the demolition and rubble removal from private residences, thus opening up spaces on existing foundations so survivors could start to rebuild their homes and quickly move out of the overcrowded tent camps.

Whenever possible, we repurposed the rubble to use as fill material to create foundations for schools, raise the slab level of flood-prone buildings, and reduce the environmental impact of rubble dumping. The scale of destruction was almost impossible to comprehend, but, as one wheelbarrow run became twenty, then forty, then sixty, and so on, a cleared foundation emerged and gradually a neighborhood revived.

Jess UK attacks rubble with vigor!

Our base was in a large concrete building next to a five-acre former cow pasture. We knew that having a big empty space was worthwhile, and we knew how to capitalize on it. In Biloxi, open space became our volunteer tent city; in Gonaives, we used it for our backpack assembly line. Léogane, as the city nearest the epicenter of the earthquake, became a hub for humanitarian relief and reconstruction. But the city lacked a central warehouse or logistical center for incoming relief agencies. We dared to dream that our empty "backyard" could fill this need.

Within a short time after our arrival, Marc had wrapped up the project in Indonesia and joined us in Léogane. He mentioned our pasture to a friend at the World Food Programme (WFP)—the largest NGO in the world—and the next thing we knew, they offered to pay the cost of improving the pasture to make it ready to set up a logistical center. The work involved laying one meter of fill over five acres of puddles and cow patties. Fill, of course, was not hard to find. We were working with units from the Canadian and South Korean armies to remove rubble, so we just asked them to dump their debris in our field. The field came alive with a flurry of dump trucks, earthmovers, and bulldozers, bringing in river rock and rubble from ruined houses to fill and level the land.

....

One of the things I said to all our partners in Haiti was, "It's my job to find a yes." That became my mantra. It was so easy to say that to people and that gave them the willingness to say, "What can we do?" We just kept finding yeses.

—Marc Young

....

Our volunteers erected a perimeter fence consisting of used shipping containers for security, and the WFP donated warehouse tents large enough to drive a truck through. With that, an unused pasture became the Joint Logistics Base (JLB), an organized and efficient hub for humanitarian aid activity. When the WFP decided to move their base elsewhere, we continued to use the field, renting the space to more than half a dozen other NGOs to which we became connected through Marc's network. In fact, the JLB enabled Habitat for Humanity and Cooperative Housing Foundation to launch their programs in Léogane, which generated paying jobs for four hundred Haitians. The rental income helped cover our own costs as we extended Project Léogane into a second year. All in all, the JLB was a phenomenal success, and much of it was due to Marc's creativity, connections, and his credibility with other organizations.

"I had a harebrained vision of what we could do with the open space, and I believed we could achieve it. But there's one outcome that I didn't predict that I'm quite proud of: the JLB employed four hundred Haitians," Marc recalled. "In a country that desperately needed jobs, the JLB—although temporary—satisfied that need. I'd never, ever thought of that outcome."

The JLB itself and the partners that used that space became trusted allies. Partnering with Habitat for Humanity, through the JLB, cemented our relationship with the organization. We carried that relationship forward to Japan, and then to the Philippines. The same relationship building happened with Cordaid (Catholic Organization for Relief and Development Aid) and the Red Cross. All Hands became a bigger player in the global aid field, all because of the JLB.

*　*　*

Back in New York, we were forging other crucial connections. In response to the earthquake, Ziff Brothers Investments (ZBI) had made a substantial donation to Partners in Health, a Boston-based nonprofit organization with a significant presence in Haiti. (The story of Partners in Health is movingly described in Tracy Kidder's book *Mountains Beyond Mountains*.) When a ZBI manager asked to see firsthand what was happening, Partners in Health referred him to us. He and his wife and daughters volunteered in Léogane, and when they returned to New York, recommended All Hands to ZBI's philanthropic arm. Two months later, ZBI gave us $250,000. It was the largest grant we'd ever received up to that point and allowed us to launch our school building program.

In Léogane alone, the earthquake destroyed 201 schools and damaged another 98. Beyond the fundamental purpose of providing an education, schools provide an important sense of normalcy and security in the aftermath of a disaster. Reopening a school not only helps puts the lives of students back on track but also enables their parents to return to work. Our model for an easy-to-build, earthquake-proof transitional school was based on a construction technique developed by Elizabeth Hausler of Build Change, which had been a huge success in our project in Indonesia.

A group of architects among our volunteers adapted the design to serve as a school building that met international standards for earthquake and hurricane resistance. Each school, with room for up to 150 students among three classrooms, could be constructed from locally sourced materials. Each building would be equipped with two biosand water filters.

David and Yaron find morning coffee time a chance for reading, planning, and friendship.

Building schools marked another step in the evolution of our organization. For our previous projects, we set a time limit of between three to six months. But in Haiti, there was so much need that six months was just too short. Rather than simply extend an arbitrary deadline, we decided to launch an extensive, goal-focused rebuild program of building thirty schools.

First day of class in one of the twenty schools we built in Haiti.

It was a huge construction project for us, but our ambitious plans had a number of unintentional benefits. Current and prospective volunteers were certain that we'd be there at least six months down the line and planned their schedules accordingly. We'd have an ongoing and evolving story of needs and deeds to present to donors. And, as our development people pointed out, it's easier to raise money to fund a specific cause, such as building schools, than just raising money in general.

Project Léogane was also a test for us: Would volunteers keep coming to help a rebuild program stretching over months—maybe even years? Approximately 1,500 volunteers offered a resounding "Yes." To achieve our goal of building 30 schools, we would have to provide a steady flow of skilled workers. So, we adapted the jobs training program we had pioneered in Gonaives: hiring Haitian workers, and training them to follow US work standards—they had to commit the night before to showing up the next morning at 7:30. If they showed up at 7:45, they couldn't work. We used the program as an opportunity to provide training in quality construction practices.

Picture a small Japanese pick-up truck. Picture loading shovels, wheelbarrows, sledgehammers, and big tools to cut rebar into the bed of the truck. Now, picture five people squeezing into a cab designed to hold two comfortably, and seventeen more hanging onto the back, and driving through muddy, wet, potholed roads to get to the project site. I was in the back, hanging on with one foot and one hand. It was just a riot.

—Mike McQueeney

Tom Jardim, an architect from Connecticut, quickly showed himself to be the man to run the school program. He came to Léogane

Little girl pauses in awe upon entering her beautiful new school.

as a volunteer and found himself drawn to where his skills could be best utilized. In the process, he fell in love with the country and committed to staying—first extending his stay for six months, then a year, then eighteen months, and ultimately more than two years. Tom learned to speak fluent Creole and became the core element in the program's success.

As Tom explained, "Building schools is actually pretty easy. It's the logistics and assessing need—the soft stuff—that's difficult." Under Tom's guidance, we had to prioritize where we focused our resources. "I interacted with school directors on a daily basis to hear from them and assess for myself the level of need," he recalled. "There were so many deserving schools and it was emotionally draining to say no to people who you know are extremely needy. I just had to get used to it, and, eventually, I became tougher and learned to trust my instincts."

One thing we learned was to shift from a reliance on our nonlocal volunteers to local crews. We wanted to empower the community, not alienate them. We found that it can create an imbalance if a relief organization is always leading the decision making and directing the work. So, Tom explained, "We hired a Haitian construction team, created apprenticeships for locals, and relied less on the school director to provide manpower. But the director would always facilitate things in the community. When you give aid," Tom learned, "there's always the potential for jealousy. That's why you don't pour all your resources into building a single, amazing school with electricity and plumbing (electricity and plumbing being atypical amenities in Haitian schools). You can't spread the wealth. Aid can cause strife—not just among locals but between locals and aid organizations." Relationships were in a constant state of negotiation and change in order to maintain positive feelings toward our group.

It typically took six weeks to construct a school, with the new one being built right next to the damaged one while school was in session. The worst of the worst of the schools we helped was a school for 300 or 350 students. Structurally, it was nothing more than a set of sticks stuck in the ground, tied together with ropes, and covered with a crazy quilt of filthy, hole-ridden tarps. It was like a dark sauna inside and, because the property was on low land, it was a muddy mess. The tables and chairs were crooked and broken. There were no bathrooms or lunch programs. Even in its derelict state, the school was *it* for the local kids. Even when the streets were nearly impassable from mud and piles of rubble, they marched to school in their bright clean uniforms. Parents were so proud of their school they wouldn't send their kids if they didn't have clean uniforms. The level of pride and commitment to education was inspiring.

There's a tremendous amount of satisfaction in building schools, providing a sustainable source of clean water, and helping people rebuild and return to their homes. That's a huge lift for the families, and the families and volunteers are motivated for each other. Still, our work took a toll. Tom explained, "In a hectic environment where you're super stressed, you can lose it, especially if you haven't had a break in a while. But as my communication in Creole got better, it got easier to put myself in someone else's place. Haiti taught me to show compassion to people at all levels and treat everyone with the same level of respect and humanness that you would your brother or your close friend."

The cholera epidemic was in full force and we'd just been hit by Hurricane Tomas, which caused a lot of flooding in Léogane. We worked eight straight days, really intense, hard work, removing mud and doing nasty work. It was a Tuesday evening and the project director said, "I can see everyone is exhausted. Who would like to take tomorrow off?" I was thinking, "Gee, I could sure use a decent rest." But not a single hand went up. Someone said, "You know, we came here to work and not to play." I was so impressed. I'll never forget that.

—Jack Ferrebee

One of the ways we could help deal with cholera was through the expansion of our biosand filter program to provide families with clean water. Designing and manufacturing easy-to-use, gravity-powered, almost indestructible concrete water filter units was another element in our overall efforts in Haiti. Eventually, we installed more than 550 filters in schools and homes. They cost nothing to run, meaning residents no longer had to spend what little income they have on water treatment tablets and can instead reinvest in their homes, their health, their businesses, and their education. Residents weren't always sure about the filters, as April Jelinek recalled. "We were coming in from the outside saying, 'You're getting sick because of something you can't see.'" To many Haitians, most of whom had little to no education, this was a foreign concept. So, she explained, "we invited local volunteers to come to the hospital and look at contaminated water through a microscope, then tell their friends and family what they saw and reassure them that we weren't crazy. Our Haitian volunteers spread the word much more effectively than we could do as outsiders."

Putting filters to use was also an important step in convincing residents of their value. "We built a few filters for one community in response to a request from a couple of residents. When we went back for a follow-up visit, a huge crowd of people came running up to us calling, 'I want one! I want one!' The initial two or three people with filters saw some improvement in their family's health; after that, everyone wanted a filter. We put filters in just about every house in that town," April explained.

Our production facility created biosand filters which provided clean water to hundred of families.

The luxury of an extended contract allowed us to think about making long-term contributions to the community. As we moved into 2011, we were accomplishing good things through the school-building and biosand water-filter programs, and there was a steady flow of volunteers. But it was obvious that what people in Haiti needed most were jobs. Helping people start and succeed in running small businesses would be a valuable, long-term contribution. As it happened, some All Hands volunteers on Project Léogane were recent MBA graduates and current students; they enthusiastically pitched in.

In the fall of 2011, All Hands launched a series of "Livelihood" programs, including courses for women entrepreneurs and young entrepreneurs, and a business basics course. (The basic business course was just that, basic: We taught, among other things, the importance of having a sign that clearly states what you offer and when you're open, if you have a business.) The courses were well attended and we held graduation ceremonies where attendees' families could proudly celebrate their accomplishments.

We held the graduation ceremonies at Joe's Bar, a watering hole run by Joe Joseph, a Haitian-American businessman who rented us the building we used for our base. Joe's Bar was Léogane's equivalent of Rick's Café American in the movie *Casablanca*: Everyone went there. Frequenting Joe's was a good way to seed more connections in the NGO community, feed money back into the Haitian economy, and give our volunteers a chance to kick back after a day of hot, hard work. Enforcing our 10 p.m. curfew wasn't a problem because Joe's Bar ran off power from our generator; we'd shut it down at 9:55 and everyone knew they had five minutes to get back to base.

Another initiative was the creation of a printed business directory for Léogane. For $25, business owners described the products and services they offered and how to contact them. Something like the *Yellow Pages* may seem obsolete to us, but Léogane had never had anything of the sort. While only somewhat useful to the intra-Léogane business community, it was very useful to the NGO community because it introduced aid organizations to Léogane-based Haitian suppliers. Making and reinforcing those connections between the local business community and the community of NGOs was a big step in helping the business community get back on its feet.

Meetings, always meetings! Experienced and talented volunteers enjoy sharing ideas.

Not everything was sunshine and success stories. As anyone who has been in Haiti for a while can tell you, there's always heartbreak lurking in the shadows. For Project Léogane, that included crushing disappointment—and a tragic death. Chris Zahuta was a first-time volunteer who had been with us for just over six weeks. He was an enthusiastic and energetic twenty-year-old who took great joy in making a difference in the lives of Haitians through his work on our transitional school program. Like many volunteers, Chris slept on top of the flat roof of our base building; it was much cooler up there than below, where people were packed eight to twelve to a room.

One night, Chris got up to go to the toilet and fell off the roof, suffering severe head trauma. After treatment at the Médecins Sans Frontières (Doctors without Borders) clinic nearby, he was flown by helicopter to Port-au-Prince, then evacuated to Miami by air ambulance. He died there on July 17, 2011. Chris's mother later told us that Chris's six weeks with us were the best of his life. He had written to her about his All Hands experience: "I love the people and the area is like nothing you could ever imagine! I love it! I'm going to make it and change someone's life." Chris's mother and brother visited Project Léogane. They left some of his ashes and we dedicated the school he had helped build to Chris's memory. His brother volunteered on the project the following year.

In 2012, we suffered another blow. We were approaching our two-year anniversary and our list of accomplishments was growing. Schools were being constructed, a new biosand filter production factory was up and running, the Livelihoods program was a hit, and we were engaged in a wide variety of programs we hoped would help the recovery of Léogane. Then, funding ran out. Although the programs were successful, we could not secure further financial grants to sustain them.

The challenge for any nonprofit organization is matching the work you do against donors' desire to fund it. To our donor base, we were viewed as a disaster response team, not a rebuilding team, and when you pass the two-year mark, the event is distant enough that it is no longer viewed as a disaster. We had seen warning signs—lagging donations—at twelve months and eighteen months that donors were moving on to supporting new events and new challenges. But we hadn't realized that a two-year anniversary, rather than cause for celebration, would mark the end of a significant amount of funding.

It's also easy for an organization to succumb to tunnel vision: You're doing good work and you're pleasing your donors, so when you submit a grant application, it's easy to assume you'll get funded. It didn't occur to us that donors might not feel an obligation to continue to fund us or that they might prefer to support someone else. The disappointment hit our staff the hardest. Many had been in Haiti for more than a year; they had helped create some of the programs and they were strongly committed to continuing them. It was difficult for them to see their cessation as anything but failure.

On March 12, 2012, we announced that we would shut down Project Léogane on April 30. We were able to complete the in-progress Livelihoods classes. We finished building twenty of the thirty schools we had hoped to build. We successfully transitioned the biosand filter manufacturing plant and distribution program to a local NGO.

Then, we sat down to do some serious thinking.

We had gone into Haiti with the plan to stay for six months; we stayed there for twenty-seven months. It *was* a very successful project, even though we didn't feel that way at the moment. We had to remind ourselves that sometimes you have to be satisfied with what you *can* do—not berate yourself for what you weren't able to do. In the disaster response business, there's a definite attitude of "when life gives you lemons, make lemonade." But the important lesson we came away with is to be aware of the depths—and the limits—of your resources and how you can best optimize those resources to solve problems. All Hands was fortunate in that we didn't have to restrict ourselves to removing rubble and rebuilding houses. We also took on projects that rebuilt a community's spirit. Those opportunities presented themselves, and we had the luxury to decide whether or not to grab them.

What we learned in our first five years of existence prepared us for Haiti. Our experience in Haiti, in turn, prepared us for the next five years.

CHAPTER 7

Serendipity as Strategy

Every disaster is different. Even though our basic response procedures were well established before and field-tested in Haiti, I'm still surprised by how often serendipity shapes our strategy and contributes to our success. That was the case in our response to the earthquake and tsunami that blasted the northeast coast of Japan's largest island in 2011.

The earthquake hit on March 11, 2011. I was in the Miami airport with Marc Young, our operations director, attending an All Hands board meeting before flying to Haiti. Pete Kirkwood, who had been instrumental in setting up our work in Bang Tao before joining the All Hands board, was with us. Pete had two brothers living in Tokyo, one of whom said that he and his family were abandoning the city because of the radiation threat from the damaged Fukushima Daiichi Nuclear Power Plant. He presented us with an available apartment if we wanted it. Marc and I changed our flights and landed in Tokyo three days later.

One of the major challenges after a natural disaster is simply accessing the affected communities. The train tracks serving the Tohoku area had been washed out; roads had buckled in the earthquake and been torn apart by the tsunami. Air travel within the region was also questionable. The day after we arrived—four days after the disaster—I was finally making progress. Through our network, we connected with a Japanese insurance company. Why insurance, you ask? Insurance adjusters must access devastated areas as soon as possible following a disaster, so they already have a transportation strategy and local contacts. Our plan was to use the insurance company to wrangle an invitation from a Tohoku community and then hitch a ride there with their adjusters.

I don't speak Japanese, and the insurance company representatives, although friendly, were not confident in their English. Fortunately for us, Henry Takata happened to be in their office that day on his own business. Henry is a Japanese-American who had attended Tufts University in Boston and worked in investment banking in the US before returning to Tokyo, where he had recently retired as a partner at Goldman Sachs. Recognizing and seizing an opportunity, the insurance people asked him to sit in on our meeting and serve as our translator.

During our meeting, Henry and I chatted about All Hands while the insurance company representative made some calls to the legislature in the Tohoku region. The representative returned with good news: "We have an invitation for you to go to the town of Ofunato. When would you like to go?" I said without hesitation, "Tomorrow." She returned to her networking contact, and Henry and I chatted for another fifteen minutes or so, until she came back.

"How many seats will you need on the flight?"

I replied we'd need three: one for me, one for Marc, and one for a still-to-be-found translator.

She returned to her negotiations, and Henry and I resumed our conversation. When she came back, she said, "We'll need names for the reservations."

In a moment of inspiration (though I did not realize it at the time), I said, "Henry, can we use your name to make the third reservation until we line up a translator?" He agreed, and the representative once again went back to her work.

"Henry," I said, as I recognized the serendipity, "your name is on the reservation. You speak English and Japanese. Want to join us?"

At that point, Henry had known me for approximately one hour. He thought my suggestion over for a few minutes. "Okay, sure," he said.

What would we have done if Henry hadn't been at the insurance company's office that day, trapped with me sharing the All Hands story? I suppose we would have found a translator, but having Henry—a fifty-eight-year-old culturally sensitive, bilingual local resident—join our team was a huge win. It was by pure chance that we were thrown together, but because we were—and because of Henry—doors opened and things began to move.

Henry Takata, "railroaded" by David, cheerfully becomes a most valued contact and volunteer.

Henry introduced us to his connections with the Goldman Sachs network as well as Credit Suisse Japan and vouched for our credibility. As a result, we became a trusted conduit for the corporate community in Tokyo. The networks of trust began to hum, and the spigots of support began to open.

Once Project Tohoku was well under way, I returned to Boston where the Fish Family Foundation had raised money specifically for Japan disaster relief. (Larry Fish's wife, Atsuko, is Japanese.) The first day I was back, they asked if I could meet with their Japan Disaster Relief Fund (JDRF) committee, which donated $50,000 to All Hands from its first round of grants.

Equally important, we received a $300,000 grant from Habitat for Humanity, with which All Hands had been an effective partner in Haiti. Although Habitat didn't have its own projects going in Japan, All Hands gave them an opportunity to contribute funds in a way that was beneficial to them and to us.

Meanwhile, because of our connection with the Kirkwood family, we were introduced into Tokyo's expatriate business community. They adopted us and hosted a successful fund-raiser for All Hands in April. By that time, we could show slides and photos from the Tohoku Project, share the impact of the donations from JDRF and Habitat for Humanity, name-drop Goldman Sachs and Credit Suisse, and generally emphasize the scope and reality of the project. The two financial grants gave us solid credibility and, as a result, we were seen by the business community as *the* trustworthy, go-to organization for aid. We raised $340,000 during the fund-raiser. The presidents of Caterpillar Japan and Morgan Stanley Japan each donated $25,000. Further, we established a relationship with 3M Japan that brought us supplies, volunteers, and generous funds. In total, we raised an additional $800,000 over the next several months and more than $1.4 million by the time Project Tohoku was completed.

In addition to gutting and rehabilitating houses, clearing sludge and debris from drainage canals, returning a fish processing plant to working status (which involved mucking out and disposing of fifteen tons of rotten fish), planting trees and flowers in a wave-razed park, reconstructing a children's playground, and restoring a temple and local cemetery so residents could grieve in peace, we took on a new and deeply satisfying task: salvaging and restoring damaged photographs.

Repeat volunteer Rebecca "Becci" Manson is a professional photo retoucher in her daily life. As she later described her work in a TED Talk, "We make skinny models skinnier, perfect skin more perfect, and the impossible possible. We get criticized in the press all the time, but some of us are actually talented artists with years of experience and a real appreciation for images and photography."

For weeks, volunteers and locals had been salvaging salt-stained photos and waterlogged albums from the muck. They'd collect them and bring them to evacuation centers in different towns in the region, in the hopes of returning them to their owners. Becci was scrubbing an *onsen* (communal bath) at one evac center when she came across a batch of photos.

Some were more than a hundred years old; some were still in the envelope from the processing lab. The vast majority of the population in our area was quite old. Their families had left the area and all that was left was the photos. I kept thinking, *If that was me, I would love someone to help me save my photos.* I couldn't help but think that, as a retoucher, I could fix that tear and mend that scratch—and I knew hundreds of people who could do the same.

I explained what I did for a living to Yumiko, the lady helping me at the *onsen*. She told the people at the evacuation center. By the time I'd finished cleaning the *onsen*, they'd set up the equipment for us and said, "Please help." So that evening, I reached out on Facebook and LinkedIn, and by morning the response had been so overwhelming and so positive, I knew we had to give it a go.

Armed with little more than a scanner and a laptop, Becci uploaded the photos to free cloud servers. Within five days, eighty photo retouchers from twelve different countries had offered to help. Within two weeks, 150 people wanted to join in.

As waterlogged, sewage-soaked, oil-scummed photos were salvaged from the ruins, they were carefully washed, then displayed in temporary libraries set up in Ofunato and neighboring towns. People would claim their photos, we would scan and upload them, and some *gaijin* (stranger) on the other side of the globe would volunteer for the job, download the photo, and fix it.

Most people think of the Internet as a place to *get* information. Within a project, though, it's a way to *propagate* information. In fact, we encourage volunteers to share what they're doing and what still needs to be done. A story may not seem very important at the time, but it may resonate, on and on like a tsunami of goodness, and build unforeseen power.

I had a concert tour that was heading to Japan a few months after the tsunami. I wanted to do some volunteer work while I was there, and, in researching ways we could connect with the community, All Hands rose to the top of my list: I didn't have a special skill set other than a pair of hands I wanted to lend, so it was perfect for me and members of my band.

My time in Ofunato was profound. I'd never been to a place where a natural disaster had occurred, and it really opened my eyes. But more than anything, the greatest impact on me was observing the steadfast dedication of the volunteers. I met people who had planned to take two weeks of vacation in Mexico with their family and opted out of that to go to Japan and volunteer for All Hands.

I was raised to believe that hard work and getting your hands dirty enriches your life. So much of the fund-raising work I do feels somewhat removed. It was a beautiful thing to be of service in a way that felt so visceral.

Doing something of service—you always hope it has its own ripple effect. That's why we decided to document my All Hands experience in a short film, *A Trace of the Sun: Volunteering in Japan* [available on YouTube]. Not everyone can get on a plane and engage in a physical way, but they might be inspired to be of service by donating a little money to enable someone else to go.

**—Sara Bareilles,
American singer-songwriter and musician**

Smiles and hugs are shared among new friends in Ofunato.

We cleaned more than 135,000 salvaged photos and digitally retouched more than 300. It's easy to underestimate the significance of snapshots until you lose everything, and especially when you lose someone. No thanks was more powerful than, "We lost our daughter but at least we have a photo of her." Restoring those bits of humanity—giving someone a tangible connection to their memories—that's what Project Tohoku was about.

CHAPTER 8

Riding a Roller Coaster Blindfolded

Anyone who has ever watched *Looney Tunes* is familiar with the cartoons in which Wile E. Coyote is running so fast that he runs right off a cliff. I felt like Wile E. Coyote in March 2012.

Japan had been a model project: Well-funded and well-run, it ended right on schedule in November 2011, six months after launch. Just a few weeks later, in mid-December, the island of Mindanao in the Philippines was blasted by Typhoon Washi (locally known as Sendong). Many All Hands folks seamlessly shifted gears from wrapping up Project Tohoku to launching Project Cagayan de Oro. Meanwhile, we were still going full tilt in Haiti.

Then, our funding crashed.

The grants we expected to allow us to continue our work in Haiti didn't come through. Our Japanese funding ended with the project. While our partnership with Habitat for Humanity in the Philippines was going well and Habitat was contributing 70 percent of the cost, we still had to raise the other 30 percent—and we just didn't make it.

When we'd examined our finances and management structure in 2010, we determined that general and administrative (G & A) expenses, i.e., the cost of day-to-day support operations, should take up no more than 20 percent of the overall funding. In order to support $50,000 per month of G & A—really a very small amount when you consider we were paying the salaries of fifteen staff members—we needed an ongoing revenue stream of $250,000 per month.

We managed to maintain equilibrium throughout 2011 with both the Japan and Haiti programs acting as funding sources. We knew there would be a definite end to the Project Tohoku funding and a possible end to Haiti funding, but we had developed an "if you build it, they will come" way of thinking and carried on under that philosophy. We had achieved a level of comfort and expectation that the status quo would continue to work for us. If we needed to run a certain number of programs to support our management needs for development and general management, well, we'd just find the funding. Admittedly, our "if you build it, they will come" thinking was a bit unrealistic, but the model had worked for us so far. Until it didn't.

We'd burned through our cash reserves in the first quarter of 2012, overstaying our limited Haiti funding. By our March board meeting, we were in a full-blown fiscal crisis. It was a heartbreaking situation. We didn't have a live project capable of generating sufficient funding for our programs *and* maintaining the organization. Darius Monsef, a stalwart supporter of All Hands since its inception in Bang Tao, Thailand, and now a member of the board, suggested that rather than keep things going, maybe we should just mothball the organization and conserve our resources for the next Big D.

We passed the hat around the boardroom table. I agreed to contribute $100,000 but asked to wait until September, the start of All Hands' new fiscal year, in order to take advantage of a generous challenge match from Lee Keet. Meanwhile, we scrounged up two $10,000 donations and one for $50,000 to hold us until then.

With little cash to spare, we had to make some very tough decisions. It was with a real sense of despair that we decided to shut down our Haiti programs. We were aware that we needed to retain key staff if we could, but we would have to cut all our other staff to the bone. Marc Young voluntarily took himself off the payroll. He'd been going nonstop for twenty-seven months, moving from Indonesia to Haiti to Japan to the Philippines and he needed a break. We had a capable project director in Chris Turner to take over for him in Project Cagayan de Oro.

About six months before we began to tighten the belt, we added Paul Burnore to the staff. I had turned seventy and we needed to build longevity and stamina into the organization—both fiscally and managerially. No one within the organization was interested in stepping up, so we looked outside and found Paul, who became our chief operating officer: He reported to me and everyone else reported to him.

Paul, a former IBM manager with extensive experience in the US, Europe, and Asia, had also worked for US AID, served two tours with the Peace Corps, and, even more significantly for us, had volunteered on two All Hands projects in Haiti. Since Paul combined corporate managerial skills and the heart of a volunteer, I hoped that he would embody our commitment to building professional management and provide the strategic smarts to help me pull us across the void and back onto sound footing.

Paul jumped in and began to craft a strategic plan for our future development. Over the spring and summer, we managed to make ends meet in the Philippines and keep alive several small domestic projects. The stress was taking its toll on all of us, but I felt like we were working our way out.

Then, on October 29, 2012, Superstorm Sandy slammed into New York and New Jersey. Sandy was not a surprise, like an earthquake or tsunami. We had ample warning of its landfall. But the size of the storm—its winds spanned more than 1,100 miles of coastline—and its timing—it hit at high tide and on a full moon—turned a serious but manageable Category 3 hurricane into a megastorm. It was second only to Katrina in the final cost of its devastation. And, because it barreled right up New York Harbor, it scored a direct strike on the most populous region of the country.

Sandy was a big Big D, and it was an opportunity for us to go big. If we wanted to secure some of the relief money to support our efforts, we needed to be seen as a major player.

Jeremey Horan, All Hands director of domestic operations, and Travis Gibson, All Hands domestic project director, arrived in New York on November 2; I arrived on November 4 (my birthday), with multiple jerry cans of gasoline loaded in my Jeep. Jeremey and Travis made a connection at Staten Island Community College and thought Staten Island would be a good geographic locus for a project.

I was thinking bigger. There were great needs in New Jersey. We also had two board members, Eric Gebaide and Adam Haber, who lived on Long Island. Eric described what people were going through there.

....

In the Rockaways, disaster response groups had gathered at the St. Francis de Sales church. It was mayhem. Local residents were coming in asking for help. Two young women who were the daughters of the local police chief were standing outside, sending volunteers in response.

These two young women were working their butts off and it was a complete mess. They'd send out a bunch of people to a particular address. One person would come back and say, "I need tools." They'd hand out some tools and the person would go back. There was lots of good will but no organization.

Literally across the street from St. Francis de Sales was a huge parking lot where a building contractor had set up camp. He had equipment and an army of big burly construction guys who knew how to use it and a tent where two women who worked in his office were trying to match work orders and projects on their laptops. But no one was coordinating their work with anyone else's.

I asked the police chief's daughters, "Have you talked to the guy across the street? No? Let me introduce you." My seventeen-year-old daughter started creating a spreadsheet, because the young woman didn't know how to use Excel. In the middle of all this, David arrived. Many of the people volunteering had worked in places where they'd seen All Hands in action. They looked at David like he was the Second Coming.

....

Brainstorming with Jeremey and Travis, I decided, "We're going to launch multiple projects —certainly one in Staten Island, but also one on Long Island. And I'd like us to do a project in New Jersey, too."

To accomplish this, we'd launch what I called the "Manhattan Project," our strategy to raise funds for our three-pronged approach to relief in the region and also, I hoped, to strengthen the organization. It wouldn't be easy since we were coming from a position of weakness. Our management team had been showing signs of strain. We needed everyone to align—and more. Just as we had proven in the field that we could thrive under stress and be creative, we needed to be aggressive and creative at the organizational level—now more than ever before.

And then, Paul called me from the Manila airport. He had been working hard to try to solve our funding issue and had fainted from stress. "I can't keep going," he told me. We determined that this role was not the right fit for Paul, and he pulled back from management responsibilities that day.

Jeremey and Travis felt they owed their allegiance to Paul because they had been working for him for nearly a year. For that reason, or otherwise, their level of intensity didn't match mine. Nor did their response match my ambition to answer the intense need in the region. They thought launching one physical project was a big deal; I wanted to launch three. We compromised with two: Project Staten Island, launched on November 8, and Project Long Island, to launch two weeks later. Jeremey agreed to head up Staten Island while Travis would lead operations on Long Island.

A few days later, as I was driving across the Verrazano Bridge from Brooklyn to Staten Island, Jeremey phoned. Travis didn't feel he could be involved in two projects and had decided to resign. I put in an emergency call to Marc Young, who came off the bench and committed to opening Project Long Island. After some discussion, Travis agreed to stay and help Jeremey, on the condition that they focus solely on Staten Island. I thought that could work, and knowing that Marc was directing Long Island reassured me that at least *that* project would be launched successfully.

We immediately contacted donors. We used our network of trust to ask people who knew us to communicate with prospective New York-based donors who knew *them*. One of our investment banking friends from Project Tohoku connected us within JP Morgan and we took advantage of their first round of funding response. Ziff Brothers Investments, which had helped us so much in Haiti, immediately kicked in $100,000.

All Hands benefitted from our reputation of parachuting into tough disaster zones and getting up to speed quickly. We had earned a top, four-star rating from Charity Navigator, a charity rating service. And the fact that we were simultaneously launching projects in two places made a powerful impression. The funds started flowing.

A note about serendipity: Because our name begins with the letter A, we're close to the top of the list on the Charity Navigator website.

And, because we have four stars, we have credibility. Consequently, when a company in Ohio that had never heard of All Hands Volunteers wanted to contribute to Sandy relief, they went to the Charity Navigator site, found us, figured we were valid, and sent us a check for $25,000.

On our own website, we pushed out the message: We're here, we can help, and we know how to do this. Prior donors stepped up. We were back in business. Still, with our cash crisis so fresh in my mind, I could not let my guard down. The last thing I wanted was to rev up two important, high-profile projects, then have to shut them down for lack of funds.

Sandy was surreal because in all other projects, I had to get on a plane. With Sandy, a couple of buddies and I jumped on our bikes, took the ferry over to Staten Island, and pedaled right to the work site.

This was our city, but it was part of our city I never would have seen otherwise: the exposure to new people and new places in your backyard; the stench of a couch that had been submerged in water and covered in mud and mold; the juxtaposition of waking up in your warm bed knowing a few miles away was an entirely different world. I was both the volunteer and the local. It made you realize that disasters can impact anyone.

—Nick Taranto

The power of *being there* took on new meaning and importance. Being where there are any potential local sources of funding makes a huge difference. I was in New York and telling everyone I contacted, "I can see you tonight, tomorrow, any day." Dirk Ziff had been on the

board of directors of the Robin Hood Foundation (RHF), a charitable organization founded by a hedge fund manager that follows its
namesake-hero's motto to "take from the rich and give to the poor."
RHF had raised $60 million for Sandy aid. I asked for an introduction.

The Robin Hood Foundation's mission is alleviating poverty, not
just in New York City but across the broader metropolitan area. They
funded us $250,000 to prototype a mold treatment response. Mold
treatment had become an increasingly pressing issue. Poor families
whose homes had been flooded couldn't afford to leave but couldn't
afford commercial remediation services. They were forced by circum-
stance, to camp out in cold, damp houses teeming with mold. Inhaling
mold spores can cause dangerous—and sometimes permanent—
breathing problems. We had a few ideas about how to help.

As Jeremey Horan recalled, we brought in a mold contractor and
paid him to create a protocol for us. We bought moisture meters
and air-quality checks and other equipment, and we implemented
our plan. It was an iterative process involving a lot of going back and
redoing homes, but it got to the point where we could get wood dry
according to industry standards. The prototype was successful, and
we proved we could remediate mold in a cost-effective manner *and
train others in our techniques.*

Mold remediation doesn't offer the same gratification as gutting
a home or mucking out a basement where volunteers can see the
change they enact with their two hands and six hours of time. Mold
may show up as black spots on the wood, or it may not show up at all.
You use a little scrubber and hose and foam, and move systematically
and painstakingly to make sure all the spaces and surfaces are covered. At the end of the day, the home doesn't look that different. The
work is exacting and tedious; you can't miss a single square inch. But
it's a necessary step in the recovery process. And after the remediation, we started doing its complement: rebuilding. We could say to

homeowners, "We tore up your floor to get to the floor joists. Now let's rebuild your floor."

Robin Hood ultimately rolled out $750,000 in additional funding to us for a total contribution of $1 million. That supported us through 2013 and allowed our work to evolve from mucking and gutting to mold remediation to repair and rebuilding.,

By January 2013, we had secured the first round of funding from the Robin Hood foundation but had no idea whether we'd hit a road-block again. It was like being blindfolded on a roller coaster; you couldn't anticipate the curves and drops nor could you know when the ride would end. All Hands had multiple, ongoing projects—not just in the US but also in the Philippines—and I was back in charge. The organization's strains from the previous year were still evident.

In February, Jeremey resigned. He had been a major contributor for years, but the strained relationship as a result of our Sandy response and his impending marriage combined to make it time for him to move on. Marc and I had an extended conversation with Travis, who agreed to stick with us for the duration of Project Staten Island. Several months later, though, he resigned too.

Through it all, Marc stayed put and held the whole thing together. And as we'd seen with the chainsaw crew in Biloxi, with the fund-raising in Cedar Rapids, and on numerous other occasions, when a void opens, people rise up from the volunteer ranks and fill it. It gave me faith during a very dark time that if we encounter a problem, our community has the creativity, confidence, and competence to find a solution. We weathered our own storm after Sandy, and we became a strong presence in Staten Island.

....

I remember coming out of one house at the end of the day. We were wearing warm clothes in addition to Tyvek suits and masks. As we were stripping off our layers, an older woman came by to ask what we were doing. Our young team leader explained and she said, "I've got the same problem. What does this cost?" He said, "Nothing." She asked, "How do I sign up?" He said, "Tell me your name and your phone number." After she did, he said, "You've just signed up. We'll be in touch and will come fix your basement." She started crying. That someone was willing to come and do that for her was beyond her comprehension.

—Mike McQueeney

By the summer of 2013, I could finally take a deep breath. The Robin Hood Foundation grant gave us high visibility, which in turn attracted more funding. In March, we started a search for someone who could replace Paul Burnore, with the understanding that he or she would succeed me as CEO. In June, we brought on Erik Dyson as executive director.

In a break from my previous candidate profile, Erik was *not* a former All Hands volunteer. In fact, he was a corporate guy like me. As he describes it, "I was working in the corporate world but had made the decision to come back to the nonprofit world." A stint with Habitat for Humanity some twenty years earlier had put the do-good bug into him. "We were posted to El Salvador, in the middle of nowhere, working to get stuff out to places where there were no roads," he recalled. "It was boots-on-the-ground and pure project management—just like what All Hands does."

After two years, Habitat asked Erik and Debbie to start its national development program in Costa Rica. "We did that for a year," he said, "then we decided that we wanted to have kids and live on more than $200 a month. I was fortunate to get into Harvard Business School, so we moved back to the US." Erik used his fellowship to Harvard Business School as a stepping-stone to the high-powered corporate jobs that would give him the managerial skills, business know-how, and financial independence to pursue his dream. "I thought I could do it in seven years," he recalled. "It ended up being fifteen years, but the goal was always there."

I was impressed that he had stuck with his plan and the board was impressed with his background. "When I decided to leave [the corporate world], I looked on the All Hands website and saw an announcement that they were looking for an executive director/CEO. I had heard about All Hands the previous year, when they were recruiting for a COO. However, I wasn't ready to leave at that point and just thought, *That's a cool organization.*" When Erik first reached out to the recruiter, the initial feedback was not very encouraging. Because he had been in the corporate world for fifteen years, the recruiter did not believe he had the skills to help All Hands. He persisted, though, and succeeded in convincing me that he was our guy. He has been a great leader for us, and it's been a pleasure to be able to speak "corporate-ese" with him as he becomes fluent in "volunteer-speak."

We were still working to get the organization recentered, but it was a much better time than the year before. And we were busy. As our Sandy efforts evolved from mucking and gutting and debris removal to comprehensive mold treatment, we came to realize that while the homes might be clear of mold, many were still severely damaged. This presented another opportunity.

In November 2013, we launched our Home Repair Program, in coordination with the Stephen Siller Tunnel to Towers Foundation and the St. Bernard Project, to address the needs of Staten Island residents still unable to move back into their homes. While we would continue to gut and demo, the majority of our efforts shifted to rebuilding homes that had already been gutted. Originally, we thought we would just install subflooring, so that the first floor of a house could become usable again. But over time, we expanded our work to include framing and decking floor systems, insulating, hanging drywall, installing cabinets, and painting—on Staten Island and Long Island.

Where would we be without whiteboards?

Both projects were very well organized and attracted many volunteers: Companies contributed teams of employees during the week and individual volunteers committed their weekends to us. There was an emerging sense of renewal, for our organization as well as the New York region's residents.

Of course, there were still plenty of frustrations. We constantly hoped that some of the millions in federal dollars allocated to Sandy response would trickle down to us, but we hadn't received any federal funding. In addition, working in New York required navigating a myriad of bureaucratic factors that were challenging, delaying, and expensive. But we kept at it. Our Sandy rebuilding efforts are ongoing through September 30, 2015, and we achieved great results.

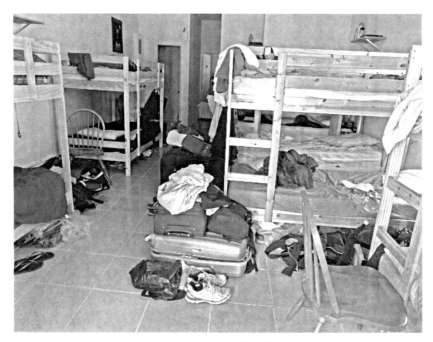

It may not be glamorous, but it's home.

Superstorm Sandy destroyed hundreds of homes and displaced thousands of people. But it gave us the opportunity to revive and reconstruct All Hands. As we helped families repair and rebuild their homes, we repaired and rebuilt our own community of staff, volunteers, and donors. There's still plenty of work to be done in New York—we subsequently launched a new project in Brooklyn—and within All Hands. But we have new skills, wider management experience, and are stronger than ever.

CHAPTER 9

A Footprint in the Ring of Fire

When I first looked into the data of disaster response, I was impressed by the different ways to measure the impact of natural disasters: lives lost, homes destroyed, schools irreparably damaged, and many others. However, the statistic that captured my interest the most was the sheer number of people affected by natural disasters: 75 percent of people who experience natural disasters live in nations encompassed by the Ring of Fire, such as Indonesia or the Philippines.

The Philippines, a group of more than 7,000-plus islands, bears more than its fair share of earthquakes, volcanic eruptions, and typhoons. So, although the Philippines is across the world from New York, it is not out of mind. Because a disproportionate part of the population in the Philippines is poor, it seemed to me that we needed to deliberately focus on that country, as well as the region as a whole.

The best approach would be to establish a permanent platform that would serve as a jumping-off point for disaster response in the Ring of Fire. We considered Bangkok, Thailand, and Jakarta, Indonesia, but ultimately decided on Manila. We'd successfully executed projects in the Philippines and the country possessed our essentials for success: an English-speaking population, a reasonable system of laws and banking, easy access for our staff and volunteers, and a vulnerability to disasters, both small and large.

All of these components—plus the search for a disaster-response project that could evolve into a multi-phase rebuilding program that would attract a steady stream of funding—were at the forefront of our minds on December 11, 2011, when Typhoon Washi dumped more than a month's total rainfall in twenty-four hours, causing flash flooding in the Northern Mindanao cities of Cagayan de Oro and Iligan. The lack of warning compounded by the flood beginning in the middle of the night made Sendong, as the storm was known locally, the deadliest of 2011.

Project Tohoku, our response to the earthquake and tsunami in Japan, had wrapped up just a month earlier, so we had an experienced team already in the region to assess damage and determine whether there was the potential for a successful project. One of our criteria for international projects is that more than 10,000 homes must be damaged or destroyed in order for us to think we will have enough impact; we also watch for events that "overwhelm a community's ability to respond." Sendong easily qualified: Government estimates put the number of persons affected at nearly 700,000, with more than 50,000 homes damaged or destroyed.

Project Cagayan de Oro (CdeO, as we soon nicknamed it) launched in January 2012, right in line with our typical thirty-days-to-launch timeline for a new project. There are three steps in shelter response after any major destruction of housing: erect tarps and tents to get people out of the weather; build transitional shelters; and, finally, construct permanent homes.

Transitional shelters are very important. Although they're meant to have a limited lifetime of up to five years, very often they're used far beyond that life span. You need to build a structure that will last. Our design uses a strong wooden frame of approximately four hundred square feet (about twenty by twenty feet) with bamboo-thatch walls and roof. Even if the thatch blows off in another storm, the structure remains and the shelter is easily repaired and reroofed.

Our volunteers loved to work on these shelters because they were quick and straightforward to build and they met an urgent need—sheltering families that had been living in tents that were vulnerable to wind, rain, and flooding. The transition shelters offer a much higher quality of life and, because they cost only about $2,500 each, we can make an impact on hundreds of families.

Building the transitional shelters came about through a partnership with the International Organization for Migration (IOM). They had the financial resources to purchase the materials and had them shipped in. But, because there is a wide gap between stockpiling supplies and actually constructing shelters, they asked us to jump in with our construction expertise. We were happy to oblige.

We forged a real prince of a partnership with Habitat for Humanity Philippines. The Philippine government had selected Habitat to manage the construction of new, permanent homes. Habitat, in turn, encouraged us to submit a bid to become a partner on the project. When we were awarded the contract to build several hundred homes, Habitat helped us understand what goes into acquiring and preparing land for permanent shelters and funded 70 percent of our costs.

Habitat's funds only covered the build of a basic housing model, but our designers wanted to build to a higher construction standard, thus increasing the cost. All Hands had to raise the money to cover the difference. This good news/bad news scenario occurred right about the time we fell off the fiscal cliff in spring 2012. Fortunately, a few years earlier, we had established All Hands Volunteers in the UK, under the strong leadership of AHV board member Ian D'Arcy. AHV UK was intended to be a European fund-raising vehicle with the express condition that any monies raised could *not* be used for projects within the United States. Funds from AHV UK, plus donations from volunteers (whom we urged to launch their own fund-raising efforts), made up the shortfall we found in upgrading the housing we built for Habitat for Humanity.

Habitat for Humanity Philippines was, and still is, a great partner. We have collaborated with them on many of our Philippines projects and hope to continue partnering with them.

We used Project Cagayan de Oro to develop our ability to blend local workers with international volunteers. We'd learned from the Haiti schools project that if you want to commit to long-term rebuilding programs, it's best to have local workers who will also commit to serve for a long period of time. Of the hundred or so people working on CdeO, about eighty were locals and forty were AHV volunteers, with ten staffers managing the operation. What was particularly wonderful about CdeO was that the workers we hired were being resettled into the homes we were building, just as Habitat for Humanity does with their homes. CdeO volunteers experienced tremendous joy, pride, and ownership (both literal and figurative) in building their new homes, just as our volunteers felt great satisfaction in building homes for their coworkers and their families.

Making the switch from cleanup and recovery to new builds was not without its own challenges. As Paul Raddant recalled, "Typically, when we do disaster response projects, we have direct contact with the beneficiary population. You go into someone's house that's been damaged by flood or tornado and you help them clean it out. You have instant gratification: You meet people and help them and they thank you. It's very powerful." But, he continued:

In CdeO, we ran into difficulty. Our volunteers were not getting that instant gratification because we were building houses in a planned new community space and there was no direct contact with the affected families. You could spend a year building fifty quadriplexes, but the only contact with the whole families was the three days at the end when we'd help them move into their new home. The most important thing for volunteers is to have that connection with community, and there was a massive disconnect.

Working side by side with the Filipino workers hired from the community beneficiaries was the main interaction our volunteers were going to get. We made the most of it. Every day, we had on-site meetings with all the volunteers and local workers to break down the tasks for the day. We'd even do morning exercises together. Imagine eighty local workers and forty international volunteers standing in a big circle doing jumping jacks and push-ups and stretching. It was a great group icebreaker.

The collegial environment on the worksite brought about another unanticipated benefit, as Paul observes. "In the Philippines, people aren't comfortable with confrontation or difficult one-on-one situations. You rarely heard a direct complaint or request; it almost always came from a third or fourth or fifth degree of separation. But we put so much focus and effort into incorporating the local workforce into the decisions and designs of the project that a year into the project, we had members of our local workforce stepping out of their comfort zone and standing up in meetings and making suggestions. I thought that was so fantastic." Paul continued, "It demonstrated a level of confidence in us and a level of buy-in to All Hands. I saw that as one of our greatest successes."

Project Cagayan de Oro lasted from January 2012 until March 2013, when we segued into Project Pagatpat. Once again, we partnered with Habitat with a similar goal of providing Typhoon Sendong victims permanent housing in safer areas. The significance of our work in Pagatpat was exemplified by a conversation between Paul Raddant and José Agbon, one of CdeO's foremen.

Paul had attended a birthday party for a local volunteer's child. José, a crotchety, older guy who rarely spoke up, told Paul he was really impressed by the houses we were building. Paul remembers, "I thought it was bizarre that he was saying something nice. So, I asked, 'Where did that come from, José?'" José responded that his house and neighborhood had been completely wiped out by Typhoon Sendong. He lost family and neighbors, and had been relocated to Pagatpat.

José lived in a house we didn't build, located on a terrace notched into a hillside. Every time it rained, mini-landslides and water poured down the hill into his house. His septic tank had been improperly sealed, so the toilet backed up and sewage overflowed into his house when it rained. His experience gave him a unique perspective from which to appreciate how much care we took to make sure similar issues didn't happen in our houses.

Paul asked José, "Do you think anything can be done in your area to mitigate this problem?" It wasn't just affecting him, but an entire row of houses—eighty families in all. José replied that his municipality had talked about putting in a drainage canal, but it hadn't been constructed. So, Paul went to check it out. He said, "the next day after work, I went to look and it seemed pretty obvious that if there were a ditch running behind the houses, it would divert rainwater and prevent flooding. I pitched the idea to Chris." Chris Turner had been on the lookout for a commemorative event to celebrate our one-year anniversary in the Philippines. Before learning of José's plight, we had been planning to go to the beach. Ultimately we decided it would be much more appropriate to celebrate our anniversary by digging a giant drainage canal. It seemed a perfect way to commemorate our year in the Ring of Fire.

Paul remembers, "That Sunday, we woke at dawn, loaded up the truck, and drove to José's neighborhood. We set up string lines, did the prep work, and spent the entire day until dark digging a two-foot wide, four-foot deep drainage canal. Dozens and dozens of our workers and their families showed up and they all jumped in to help. We had twenty kids under six appear and insist on helping. As volunteers removed dirt from the trench, we filled countless bags with the dirt. Our small army of children carried off the dirt bags for us. Not only were we able to dig the trench but all the dirt was taken off site the same day. There was no trace of us having been there except a perfectly edged trench. That was my best day in the Philippines—working my ass off with friends and neighbors, doing something good for people," Paul said proudly.

From that day forward, José, who had been the most crotchety—even angry—guy, completely changed the way he approached the AHV workforce and the work we were doing. From then on, any time one of our workers had a difficulty, José would be the guy who would come to Paul and say, "Hey, we should do something about it." It was a remarkable transformation.

We built more than 550 transitional shelters and 300 permanent homes in the Philippines, and we tightened our ties with Habitat. Our staff accumulated substantial experience of the working culture and how to interact with local laborers. The combination of our tremendously positive experience and the large number of volunteers who signed on to work with us convinced All Hands Volunteers that the Philippines was the right place to establish an AHV Southeast Asia base. We made the decision late in 2012 and incorporated All Hands Philippines.

A 7.2 magnitude earthquake rocked the Visayas region of the Philippines on October 15, 2013, just as we were wrapping up Project Pagatpat. More than 73,000 structures were damaged, at least 14,500 of which were completely destroyed. Because we were already in the country, our All Hands response team landed on the ground within twenty-four hours of the earthquake to set up Project Bohol. Once again, we collaborated with the IOM to distribute shelter repair kits, underscoring the advantages of sustaining and strengthening these productive partnerships in the region.

Less than a month later, on November 8, one of the most dangerous typhoons on record crashed into the Philippine island of Leyte and neighboring islands in the same Visayas area. When it slammed ashore, Haiyan (known locally as Yolanda) measured the highest reported wind speed of any typhoon in history. It did massive damage: More than *one million* homes were destroyed or severely damaged. Clearly, this was a very Big D.

Because we were working in the neighborhood, so to speak, we responded quickly. Within a week, the AHV assessment team had arrived to survey the damage, reach out to our partner organizations and local communities, and determine how and where All Hands' response could best meet the greatest need. The city of Tacloban on the eastern shore of Leyte was receiving the most media attention, so we chose Ormoc, a smaller city on the western shore and accessible by ferry from Cebu, as our initial base.

With sufficient staff in the country, we could continue to manage Project Bohol while we launched Project Leyte, but we transferred Marc Young, our most experienced response coordinator, from Bohol to Leyte. The devastation from Haiyan was so vast, with houses flattened and trees snapped to the ground all along its path, it left behind a veritable moonscape marked only by huge piles of rock and rubble. We knew immediately that Project Leyte would be a multiphase response extending over several years.

After months of deconstruction in Ormoc, we shifted our focus toward long-term recovery, concentrating on temporary and permanent homes. Once again, we collaborated with IOM, as well as new partners like Operation Blessing, CRS, Samaritan's Purse, and Gawad Kalinga. We also worked with the San Miguel Foundation, the charitable arm of the largest food, beverage, and packaging company in the Philippines and Southeast Asia. Through our partnership with SMF, we rebuilt a school in the area of Tabango, providing a safe learning environment for 295 children.

Down in action

Interacting with kids is part of the All Hands way.

As Project Leyte evolved, we reached out from Ormoc into other areas of need on the island. Ongoing projects provide All Hands with a way to absorb our experienced staff and a compelling story with which to engage our donors. Engaging donors, whether new or long-term, is difficult to do if your organization is always speaking in the past tense. We're now in our third year of projects in the Philippines and presently talking with Habitat, San Miguel, and the Philippine government to fund the construction of hundreds of permanent shelters in the country. We expect to stay busy there beyond 2015.

The Philippines have seen us through a lot of changes in the past three years. One of the biggest involved Marc Young. You might recall that Marc kicked himself off the payroll in April 2012 to help us cut costs and to give himself a well-earned break. But he barely had a chance to catch his breath when Superstorm Sandy occurred and he took on Project Long Island. Marc does really well in the chaos of a crisis. In the early days, when a project required two to four months of intense activity, Marc would work intensely and then take off for a few months to recharge his batteries. Then he broke his rhythm and put in twenty-seven months straight on our projects in Indonesia, Haiti, and Japan.

Work boots and gloves are left outside to help keep our base (living quarters) clean.

As Project Leyte got underway, it was clear that Marc was running on fumes. With strong, experienced staff ready to step up, he voluntarily pulled himself off the payroll again in December 2013. He was an incredibly valued member of our team who, though not currently on staff, is available for other projects should we need him.

Another change brought on by Haiyan is that we moved ahead with our commitment to establish a Southeast Asian base in the Philippines. While we're incorporated in the Philippines, we don't yet have a dedicated physical space. Still, we've always known that our real "base" is not a physical place, but our people. From the earliest days of the "Darius, Marc and David show," we knew that if we had the right people, the rest would follow.

Paddy Durrant, our new Director of International Assessments and Disaster Response, is now our "man in Asia." A seasoned All Hands alum, Paddy volunteered in Gonaives (Haiti) and Sungai Geringging (Indonesia), and then led our biosands filter program for Project Léogane in Haiti. After Léogane, he took a break to earn a degree in disaster management. He's based in Southeast Asia, and he can reach into any of our Philippines projects to pull from our ever-deeper pool of experienced AHV staff whenever he needs to assess a disaster.

Paul Raddant is our new Director of International Recovery and Rebuild. Paul heard about All Hands while working with a hospital in Haiti following the 2010 earthquake. When his four-week volunteer tour on Project Léogane turned into four months, Paul officially joined the All Hands team, managing the construction of twelve schools in Haiti and continuing as a key member of our rebuild projects in CdeO and Staten Island. After Paddy has assessed a potential

Our girl gang choreographed mixing concrete for footers for a home in Tacloban.

project and we approve it, Paul steps in to launch it and keep it running smoothly.

Each and every one of our projects is special in its own way, but Project Leyte stands out for attracting new volunteers from everywhere in the world. People came from fifty-eight different countries, including Nigeria and Chile. They shared a strong desire to help, and we're fortunate they found us. We were—and still are—the only organization I know where you can volunteer without having special skills and without having to pay for the privilege. All you have to do is be there. Being there has even greater resonance for us as an organization. Because we were there in the Ring of Fire, with projects in Indonesia, Bangladesh, Japan, and now our third year in the Philippines, we have established a strong foundation from which to help people in need.

CHAPTER 10

The Money Behind the Magic

Jack Ferrebee began volunteering with All Hands on Project Gonaives when he retired from his law firm. "My very first experience made me decide to donate," he explains. "When I saw that the money from donors was going directly to the community, I knew this was an organization I wanted to support financially and be a part of." Now a member of the All Hands board of directors, Jack can't wait to get back out into the field. "I really want to get back to volunteering," he said. "All Hands will be my second career for sure."

Many All Hands donors have followed Jack's path: They may have initially responded to one of David's periodic pleas for support because they knew and admired him. But as soon as they got their hands dirty working on a project, supporting All Hands became a personal issue. Here's how they describe what they do and why they do it.

The Power of Being There

Volunteers aren't the only people whose lives are changed as a result of helping out. When donors see the impact their support has—not just in helping devastated communities rebuild but also in building something inside All Hands volunteers—something shifts deep inside. Atsuko Fish, cofounder, Japanese Disaster Relief Fund and All Hands volunteer, explained her epiphany: "I can change people's lives? There is nothing better than that. When you can connect people to people, it's a very powerful experience. It makes me a better human being."

Atsuko continued: "I started the Japanese Disaster Relief Fund on March 12, 2011, one day after the earthquake and tsunami, and raised $150,000 from people in the Boston area by March 14. I gave All Hands $60,000. My principle is that when I use people's money, I am accountable to make sure the money is properly used. All Hands believes you have to be there, and I do, too. I'm too old for physical work but I needed to be there to see it." So Atsuko traveled to Tohoku, where a huge fish factory had been badly damaged by the tsunami. With no electricity, its huge industrial refrigerator had broken down and the contents were rotting. She remembers, "The smell of dead fish was unbelievable. One day, a local delegation asked, 'Do you think you can help us clear out the refrigerator?' We had no idea what we would find inside. After a long silence, a volunteer said, 'I came here to help. I'll do it.' Then others stood up: 'I'll join.' 'I'll join.' Everyone said, 'We're here to help, no matter what. Let's do it.'" That's the All Hands vision and mission—volunteers step up to help the people who need help.

Atsuko observed about the All Hands experience in Japan, "At first, the people in Tohoku didn't want foreign help. This is a part of Japan that's not exposed to foreign people. Their basic attitude is, 'What do they want? Why are they helping us?' The volunteers didn't care; they just started cleaning up. Little by little, trust began to build in each other. At the end," she continued, "the whole city understood why the foreigners came to help and what it means to help each other. And they were so appreciative. Once you experience heartfelt gratitude, there is nothing better." Although Atsuko could not contribute physically to the response, she facilitated the distribution of tremendous financial assistance. "Money builds the people-to-people connection," she explained. "Many All Hands volunteers have taken a break from traditional schooling, but someday they will be leaders of society because they understand pain in the human experience. Someone who knows that pain will become a real humanistic leader. All Hands gives them that opportunity."

Mike Pehl, a donor, board member, and volunteer, echoes Atsuko's observations. "I look to donate money to things that are meaningful, so I can see that my donation has a direct impact. I can donate to any organization in Boston, and I do, but it's never clear what happens to the money. In the case of All Hands, I know what's going to happen to the money. All Hands provides help when it's most needed, and that's what makes the organization exciting to me." Like Atsuko, Mike has been on site and experienced firsthand what the feeling is like.

I volunteered in Léogane twice, once with my oldest daughter and the second time with my son and oldest daughter. I used the opportunity to check out the project. You quickly figure out that All Hands is a very special organization, and it is because of the volunteers—their commitment, what they're willing to do, the day-to-day direct impact they have on the communities they serve. It's absolutely remarkable. And they do it every day!

He sums it up: "Every day, you're making a meaningful impact. That's why it's a life-changing experience."

Erik Dyson, All Hands Executive Director, says, "We not only want people to see our work, we *need* them to see our work because we are so different from much of the disaster response or rebuild world." He continues:

> The difference is that we don't come in with a predefined idea of what we do. We show up in a community and we say, "What do you need? We've got forty people willing to work like dogs. What can we do for you?" Locals don't believe us at first. They wonder, "Are you trying to convert us? Going to charge us?" But we build credibility very quickly. Then, ideas start to occur to us, because we're out in the field every day with passionate, smart people asking, "What else does this community need?"

"Sometimes," he observes, "it's obvious. They need houses, so we build houses. Sometimes, it's not so obvious." After Typhoon Haiyan, AH volunteers pulled Erik aside and said "You know what is the passion in this community? Basketball." The local basketball court had been destroyed but the volunteers had met a welder, who offered to repair the basketball court if they brought him the materials. The volunteers took the ball and ran with it. They said, "We'll put it together and paint it on our days off, but it'll cost $1,500 in materials." They asked me, "Can we fund it?" My answer, without hesitation: 'Absolutely!' The fact that we can have people thinking like that and that our teams can make those decisions to have that kind of impact on the community is what makes us different."

All Hands is not hemmed in by "we can only do this or that." Sometimes, we need the discipline to decide which things we do well and which require a skill set that our volunteers don't have. But we can have that conversation on a regular basis. That's what sets us apart: We're flexible, nimble, and ready to act. Erik says, "I can't write in our annual report that we put a basketball court in San Niño, but I guarantee that the community will remember the basketball court we built for them more than eighty-five transitional shelters we constructed. They needed it and we could do it, and if we didn't do it, nobody would."

Michael McQueeney, donor, board member, and volunteer from the very beginning of the organization, really puts his finger on the All Hands magic.

. . . .

When David was in Thailand [in 2004], I was on the list of folks he asked to send money. I joined the board before I went on a project, so I had different reasons for getting involved. What I originally liked about the model was the connection between dollars contributed by donors leveraged by hours committed by volunteers.

I understood the organization differently after I volunteered. I was blown away by the flexibility and efficiency of what actually happened in the field. I saw the business model live and in action and understood better why people want to go to a place like Haiti, live on rice and beans, work like dogs, and get up and do it again six days out of seven. It was a revelation.

What makes All Hands so special is that it's nonbureaucratic, very flexible and there's a complete lack of ego. We just try to figure out how to help people in a situation given the resources we have. I've seen a lot of other volunteer organizations where there's a lot of bureaucracy and a lot of silliness. We don't have that. We've got a willingness to learn and continuously improve, but we're all about trying to help in a practical manner.

That shows up in spades on some of the littlest projects. Sometimes, we'll just send people on site to help local people coordinate the response. We've got knowledge about managing disasters that, if it's not unique in the world, is certainly rare. We've developed a series of different playbooks—because every disaster is different—and we've tried to learn and be more effective going forward.

....

Experiences like Atsuko's, Erik's, and Michael's are what gets donors interested in All Hands. And the best way to get them engaged is to get them out on a project. People become amazing advocates when they see it and touch it.

The Method Behind the Magic

Although many of the donors and staff sound inspired when they talk about the All Hands magic, they are also pragmatic businesspeople. It's their ability to see All Hands as a business that allows them to fulfill its mission.

"At first, I was a lone wolf," says Nick Taranto, "just trying to see how I could help and get involved." He remembers:

....

I was so impacted by the work being done, I wanted to share that with others. That's when I brought down Dartmouth students and Harvard Business School students and friends from all over. Now, I'm a father and have my own business, so I can't jump on a plane. But serving on the board allows me to move from wolf to shepherd to make sure the organization is well-funded and the strategy is spot-on, and that we have the right people on payroll who do the day-to-day tending of the flock.

As a board member, Nick's job is to make sure the organization has enough money so that when a disaster occurs, All Hands can respond quickly and effectively. "Basically," he says, "we make sure our mission is well-defined so that we don't end up doing everything for everyone."

One of the current driving goals of the All Hands board is to build and reinforce the foundation so that All Hands can be a self-propagating stand-alone organization moving forward. "Our goal," Nick says, "is to put that foundation in place so that the health and longevity of the organization are not solely reliant on David and his generosity and his friends to keep the mission alive."

The biggest drive is the endowment: raising enough funds so that future projects can be funded out of an investment rather than on an ad hoc basis. The unfortunate reality of disaster response is that the best time to raise funds is in the immediate wake of the disaster. "The bigger the disaster," Nick notes, "the more headlines it makes, the more people will respond. But it's about building a fund-raising organization that can take advantage of that and extending its reach." Once the disaster is no longer in the headlines, the funds dry up. Making sure the endowment is well capitalized is imperative.

Lee Keet, a longtime donor and volunteer, offered me good advice during the All Hands fiscal crisis of 2012. "David," he said, "you need to think about succession—the stability of the organization—so when you hire people they know they can be paid and will stay. You need a more strategic approach to *your* business." Lee encouraged the creation of an endowment that can also be used as an emergency fund.

He explained, "It should be a couple of million dollars to start and then can grow," and then he made us an offer we couldn't refuse. "I'll make you a challenge for the first million. You find the second million and I'll be there." It took us three years, but we finally made it in 2014.

The All Hands endowment, like its volunteer workforce, is built off any level of contribution. Sizable donations are wonderful and game-changing for us. But if someone's son or daughter comes back and said, "That is the most amazing thing I've ever done," and they give us $100 for next ten years, that's wonderful, too. Erik says, "I'd rather have one thousand $100 donors than one $100,000 donor. It gives us greater reach around the world and makes us more sustainable." And, as Ian D'Arcy says, "It's great to be on project, but it's good to have a way to continue to help when you're back in the real world." All Hands hopes its supporters will give in whatever way they can.

Jack Ferrebbee observes, "I think we're getting better at nurturing donors. After Project Léogane, we tracked donors and let them know if they donated $100, we could provide clean water to a family of four in Haiti for ten years. We could remove the fear of cholera from their lives. That got a lot of bounce because it was $100 and many folks could say, 'If I can provide clean water to a family of four for ten years for just $100, I'll do it.'" From there, All Hands scaled up for schools. Jack recalls approaching people who could afford to donate more and proposing, "For $25,000 we can build *your* school, with a plaque with your name on it." In that way, All Hands further connected our donors to our work. They had a tangible piece of our labor. We managed to build twenty schools with the money we raised.

For Mike Pehl, it's a pretty straightforward equation. "The minute we get people to our projects and they understand what we do, they become lifelong friends. That's the trick in fund-raising: Find people who get emotionally involved and make this their primary charitable activity. Still," Mike says, "fund-raising will continue to be a critical issue for All Hands."

$$\$100 \times 10 \text{ years} = \$1000$$

....

The historical model was that a need arises, we put a lot of people to work, spend a lot of money on the activity, and then the need is gone, and you're back to zero. But the problem is, you can't scale the organization up and down from zero to a couple hundred people to zero. There's a baseline cost you have to cover. One thing the organization has to do is have a fund-raising capability to sustain itself. That's the first law of our business: Keep ourselves in business so you can react to an event.

We must have a rainy day fund and build up an asset base. The best way to get baseline assets is by getting grants from corporations that will commit to baseline funding in the absence of a project because we're doing great things.

....

Whether you call it a rainy-day fund or endowment, it's a financial foundation that sustains the entire All Hands organization. With that support in place, we can focus on securing project-specific funding when a disaster occurs.

As in any business model, repeat "customers" help sustain us; in our case, our customers are our volunteers. Now, in our tenth year, we have an ever-increasing network of people who provide support on an ongoing basis and who will be there as we launch new projects. This base of support enhances our ability to move quickly on new efforts, like our 2015 Nepal earthquake response, so that the broader public community can see us engaged quickly and in a bold fashion. It also helps a lot that we've earned the highest ratings from organizations like Charity Navigator and Guidestar, since many potential volunteers look to those sites for guidance. And through it all, our volunteer alumni base keeps growing, forming another support column in our overall foundation.

CHAPTER 11

The Good (for Nothing) Club

Because I ran All Hands Volunteers out of my home for its first eight years, everyone I knew was exposed to our mission—highly exposed. We've held board meetings in the living room and management meetings around the kitchen table and had countless All Hands volunteers camp out on our couches and beds and floor. As a result, there's a strong sense of attachment between my extended family and the All Hands family. (So much so, in fact, that my daughter and her husband celebrated their fifteenth wedding anniversary volunteering at Project Léogane in Haiti, and seventeen members of our extended family spent Thanksgiving 2012 helping on our Sandy project.)

My family recognizes and identifies with the basic goodness of All Hands: There's a reason to be affected by and connected with what's going on in the world. And they recognize the impact All Hands has had on me. It has given me a real purpose.

I remember thinking during my days in business that if you are utilizing all of your skills, you're in the right job. All Hands has called

on every skill and capability that I have and some I didn't know I had, as well as demanding some I didn't have. It's stressful, demanding, difficult, satisfying, productive, creative, and meaningful work. It scratched an itch I never knew I had—to do good in the world.

I love the problem solving. The problems we face are so immediate and so complex, but if you talk to enough people, solutions will emerge. And when you deliver something to people who have nothing, their gratitude is immense. It's so uplifting to the volunteers and the community that something is being accomplished—even if we're just clearing a playground so children have a safe place to play. I love it when people whose lives have been blasted apart by a natural disaster realize that someone cares enough about them to help them build a path back to normalcy. As All Hands volunteers, we never know how far we can accompany them on that path, but we do our best to help them get well on their way.

What I love most of all is that so many of our volunteers and donors discovered—sometimes to their surprise—that they feel the same way, and that All Hands provided them the opportunity to make a transformative discovery.

I often ask our volunteers, "What's important to you in your life?" Were I to answer my own question, I would say "purpose." That's why it was so rewarding to accept the 2014 Purpose Prize, which recognizes people who, at any moment of their life (in my case, at some point when they're over sixty) launch a new enterprise just to help people, on behalf of All Hands Volunteers. I love the concept of the prize, and I'm so proud of what it says about our volunteers and staff. In recognizing and validating what we do, the Purpose Prize also challenges All Hands to strengthen our platform going forward. In addition to the congratulations, there were underlying questions, "What are you going to do next? How will All Hands move into the next ten years?"

Strengthening Our Foundation

When Erik Dyson took over the direct management of All Hands on July 1, 2013, I shifted into the role of chairman. I see that role as allowing me to focus on what we must do to make us a strong and sustainable organization.

Having survived the many soars and swoops of funding volatility, one of my immediate commitments was to bring us a measure of financial stability. The first step was to raise the money for a $2 million Impact Fund. The idea originated with Lee Keet, one of the original Super Friends group, whom I reached out to back in 2007 with a Hail Mary plea to donate $50,000 over the course of two years. Being asked to become a Super Friend pushed Lee and his wife to volunteer with Project Pisco in Peru, and the experience made him a great supporter as well as a source of financial aid.

In 2011, Lee offered to match donations up to $1 million for what we named the Impact Fund. It's not an endowment fund, because I want the ability to raid it if necessary; nor is it a rainy day fund, either, because I don't want it to be just for emergencies. It's something altogether different.

Lee's offer was strategic and catalytic: It forced us to think differently and it galvanized us into action. The Impact Fund is a way for us to achieve stability, but it also enables us to be strategic and catalytic in our actions: If we see a chance to make a positive impact, we can step in immediately without first having to scramble for the funding. When Erik joined in 2013, I took on the task of matching Lee's offer as a major challenge. We announced its successful completion in June 2014.

Securing our Impact Fund was like a start-up business winning a big contract. It was a game changer. All Hands is not unlike a start-up. I've worked on—and served on the boards of—several start-ups. They're fun. They're intoxicating. But if you want a start-up to succeed, at some point its staff must hit rock bottom and sober up.

We went through our detox during our 2012 cash crisis. Now we're at a strengthening point: We're gathering people and installing processes to be ready for our next phase of growth.

In a small business, you know you're on the path to profitability when you reach the point where you can hire sales staff to boost the amount of cash flow. In the disaster business, you must have projects that bring in enough money to pay for more fund-raising.

Here's one simple but significant equation: Charity ratings organizations believe you should spend less than 10 percent of your revenue on fund-raising. So, if you hire a development person (that's the industry term for fund-raiser) at an annual salary of $50,000, how long will it take them to raise $500,000? That's a really challenging step on the path to sustainability, since we don't have a broad set of prospects for a new development person to approach.

Here's another unpleasant, but important, algorithm: As you gather more knowledge, losing it becomes more expensive. It didn't bother me that, after Biloxi, 1,500 volunteers went back to their previous lives because we kept the two we thought most valuable: Darius and Marc. But our subsequent big projects in Haiti and Japan were essentially universities for accumulating on-the-job wisdom on disaster response. When those projects ended, we "graduated" many people with postgraduate degrees, but we lacked the structure and funding to give them the security they needed to remain with us.

Of course, it's part of the life of small challenging organizations that people flow through them. Marc describes it as "the biological window of opportunity": Young people go all out for a year or two, but then something happens—they get married, they have kids, their significant other finds a solid job and wants to settle down—and the window slams shut. That's especially true when there's financial uncertainty: People are loath to commit too much to you when you can't commit too much back. Part of the lifecycle or not, limiting the negative impact of the biological window of opportunity, especially as it relates to salaries, was of paramount importance to the sustainability of All Hands.

At annual revenue levels between $1 million and $2 million, as we painfully learned, we were unstable. At our current funding level of $3 to $4 million a year, we've managed to achieve a degree of equilibrium. We would be even more stable at $5 million.

That's led us to make different strategic decisions: to take on longer-term projects, which, in turn, necessitate a different execution model requiring different skills and management experience. Of course, we fully intend to stay true to our core mission of providing immediate response to natural disasters.

We're trying to prove we can do both. Meanwhile, our model has continued to evolve in unusual and unusually satisfying ways. We have become successful in coaxing some of our corporate supporters to visit our projects, and we're confident that will help to strengthen our long-term relationships.

A Good "Do" Partner

All Hands has proven that it deserves a place at the table in disaster response and recovery. It's a big deal that a volunteer-based organization can become such a reliable and dependable resource in communities hit by disasters. Part of that recognition comes from going in to an area with the inherent flexibility and creativity that comes from not having a predetermined notion of what we're going to do. And we can stay for as long as there's volunteer interest and donor support—we stayed for two years in Haiti and even longer in the Philippines.

Our flexibility distinguishes us from multiple other disaster organizations. It also gives us a different lens through which to look at a community early on and anticipate what its needs might be. What we can bring to a community during the initial response to a disaster

AAV ⇒ partner with "money-accessible" organizations (e.g. IOM
⇒ integrated locals into projects by training them, paying them
ALL HANDS
⇒ blending local + int'l volunteers
⇒ developing + nurturing relationships with community leaders

provides a strong foundation as the community begins to recover. As importantly, our low-cost model makes us a good "do" partner for other organizations that may be more successful at fund-raising. Our excellent execution capability makes us a good partner in general. And, particularly on international responses, our model gives us the ability to integrate local community members into our workforce, pay them a decent daily wage, increase their skills, and create a unique cultural experience by blending local community workers and our volunteers.

When we're there from the beginning, the community knows us. They accept us at a moment of need, and we work tirelessly to establish very strong relationships with community leaders. For example, it's always a challenge to decide which families should get a new home when so many homes have been destroyed. Through our relationships with community leaders, we trust them to select the families who can most benefit from our aid.

Relationships with community leaders also allow us to be connected to the local government. Being there early and promising to stay after other organizations pack up their tents sends a very powerful message to a mayor of a community that's been hit by a major disaster. It gives us a working partnership. We can act as influences in identifying not only the greatest need but also the greatest *unmet* need. If the local officials can direct us toward one unmet need and we can provide a solution, it's a powerful opportunity for that community.

The greatest unmet need, typically, is shelter. Often, residents don't want to reconstruct their community in its original location because of the risk of future disasters. Whole communities must be relocated. Shifting people out of tents and into transitional homes that are safe for five or ten years is where we make a lot of headway. It's a huge, important task and the scale is staggering: The number of homes needed after major events like a typhoon or hurricane or earthquake is in the hundreds of thousands.

When we arrive, we know it will take an extended period of time to meet these needs: If you're resettling a community, you must find land, prepare the site, and build homes while selecting the beneficiaries who will live in those homes. We know that we can't do that in just a few months. We must commit for an extended period of time.

Having extended programs is as good for our organization as it is for the community. If we can find cost-effective ways to meet those needs that also match our donor requirements, we can be one of the few organizations that will remain beyond the first year post-disaster. If we identify the right places and the right teams to deliver the right product or service, we can manage overlapping rebuild projects going on in several areas of the world. The donor dollars required for rebuilding aren't as available as those for immediate disaster relief, but the need is just as great. The challenge is making certain that we continue to find necessary work—and that we find funding sources to cover our work after the news crews move on.

And there's even more. There's a whole field of disaster risk mitigation, like planting trees to prevent flooding and landslides. It's something we can do in the gaps between natural disasters. We can use our expertise to be effective and establish relationships that will help everyone when a disaster strikes.

Search and Connect

We can further leverage our strengths as a connector to other organizations by helping *them* be more effective in meeting their goals.

When we land in a disaster area, the first thing we do for our volunteers and staff is create a safe shelter with a supply of food and water, power, a place to sleep, internet access, and connections with the local community. That's a solid platform from which others who might want to try out a project could benefit. As we did so well in Haiti with our Joint Logistics Base, we could accelerate other NGOs' ability to connect into the community.

Let's say someone wants to help restart an agricultural economy by discussing alternative crops and planting techniques. Or, perhaps there are structural engineers who want to explore ideas for safe, durable, and affordable housing. We could invite them to live at our base, where they can take advantage of safe and easy access to the local community. We could help to eliminate a lack of confidence that stems from unfamiliarity that may prevent some talented people from jumping in. From the beginning, as Darius Monsef said, "We conveyed the sense of a safe, secure, sensitive, creative, active community." We still do—and we want to share it with other aid organizations.

It's a search-and-connect role: looking beyond what we can do to other community needs and finding other NGOs that can partner with us or use us as a launch pad for related projects. We can stand out by being an NGO that helps others do their jobs.

It's even possible that we engage in projects that aren't triggered by natural disasters. For example, there's now a recognized need in West Africa to build community health clinics in areas that were hit by the Ebola virus. Might we have an interest in that? It's certainly something we have the skills to do. If we can evolve to the point where we can bring our staff and volunteer resources to development projects in areas of significant need, we could have continuity between natural disasters and further leverage our unique strengths as an organization.

In short, as we build on our first ten years and look to the next, there's a wide world with many possible paths to explore. But it's not so easy to take that first step. It's like starting a new career: How did you get your first job? We haven't gotten our first job in the search-and-connect capacity yet. But it's something I think would be good for us to develop.

One thing won't change as we look ahead to our next ten years: We will not ask our volunteers to "pay to play." Erik Dyson explains why, recounting his own learning curve.

"I quickly concluded that the All Hands model was flawed in the sense that we don't ask our volunteers to contribute financially," he recalls of his early days with AHV. "In my Habitat for Humanity days, we periodically hosted volunteer work camps. When the volunteers left, they'd leave a $4,000 donation, which covered the cost of a house." Erik thought he could simply apply that paradigm to All Hands. He continues:

> During one of our many All Hands conversations about money and sustainability, I said, "There's an easy solution. If it costs $25 a day per volunteer to run the project, charge everyone $25 a day." I floated it by a few staffers and they cringed, perceiving every negative stereotype about a businessperson—I was coldhearted and just out to make money.
>
> I wasn't easily deterred, so I decided that every time I'd visit a project, I'd float the idea by the volunteers. Some said, "Okay, we can deal with that." Some said, "You're the antichrist. This would kill the organization."
>
> I was in the Philippines on top of a jeep coming back from work when I asked a young British architect what he thought. He said, "Erik, it doesn't matter whether you charge me $5 or $25. *You've now changed this to a transaction.* You're now a hotel, a restaurant. Every person's level of expectation will change because now it's a business transaction. And it's not as if it's a good hotel because I had to sleep in a room with three other people, with no running water, and eat rice three times a day."

That conversation had a profound impact on Erik, showing him that what we do is not transactional. We create an opportunity for people to have direct, person-to-person experiences. As Erik concludes, "I'm convinced that people walk away from All Hands and their life has been changed in some way. Some people will feel compelled to help by giving us money. Some won't, and that's fine. But once we change to 'you have to pay to play,' we become a boardinghouse. That's not what we're going to be."

Celebrating in Mattapoisett. Finally, the office is out of our house and into a real office space.

The Good (for Nothing) Club

A lot of people say, "Oh, you run an NGO—it must be great to be doing good for people!" It is. But along with many moments of great satisfaction and uplift, there are hundreds of hours of difficult planning, belt-tightening budgeting, campaigning for funds, and wondering, "Oh, hell, do I really have to do this?"

Running a for-profit company was, in all actuality, much easier. We could write a strategic plan for revenue growth and maintain a high degree of confidence that it would succeed.

With All Hands, I can't look ahead and see where or when we'll have a new project. The best I can do is ensure we have the capability to deal with whatever needs arise: management capability, volunteer capability, and donor capability.

That's why our rebuilding projects are so important for us. Now that we've proven the model, our responsibility is to expand and enrich it, maybe in the ways we've envisioned and maybe in ways that have yet to emerge. But the model must be strong enough to bridge the gaps between Big D disasters.

Donors will not fund us in a standby capacity. Volunteers want to schedule us on their calendars. After the initial media buzz of a natural disaster, a multiphase rebuilding project gives us a profile demonstrating lasting impact and helps donors grasp the power of what we do.

As we go forward, our choice of which disasters we respond to will be influenced by whether we can find donor interest in both the short- and long-term. We want to be in the position of always having an ongoing project in both the US and internationally. We'll just be more measured about turning the rheostat up and down on where to go and how much to engage.

Ours is a pretty complex business, frankly. But we muscle on. People are so drawn to our model that it persists in spite of the tumult and change.

I like to call All Hands the "Good (for Nothing) Club"—as in, people who are willing to "do good . . ." for "nothing." While most organizations shy away from using spontaneous unaffiliated volunteers and tell them to stay home and send money, we invite them to join us and welcome them enthusiastically when they do. (Just be aware that while our welcome is warm, the bucket showers are cold.) We've taken on the responsibility of organizing volunteers in a way that eliminates any burden on our host community, creating a flexible and adaptive workforce whose energy knows no bounds.

* * *

In 2004, I imagined the next ten years of my life as a combination of serving on corporate boards and advising and investing in young companies, sprinkled with a nice dose of leisure—a conventional path for a CEO easing into retirement. To be honest, I didn't think too much about it. I was sixty-three at the time and serving on boards seemed a good way to carry me through the next decade.

Then serendipity struck. If I hadn't been a board member of Tektronix, I wouldn't have met Tim Tse. If I hadn't met Tim Tse, my response to the 2004 Indian Ocean earthquake and tsunami would probably have been limited to some horrified expressions of sympathy. Maybe I would have donated money. I certainly wouldn't have packed up and traveled to Thailand. I could never have dreamed of how the next ten years would unfold or how much they would change me.

I'm still involved with a few corporate boards but that's coming to an end. After you've been on a board for a while, you're usually asked to leave to make room for new blood. That's fine with me. It's probably also fine with some of my fellow board members, who would much prefer to chat about their golf scores or travel plans than hear why poverty is a force multiplier for damage in a natural disaster.

What I'm doing is very different and I'm convinced it's better, definitely for the world—certainly for the thousands of volunteers who have come back with new ideas about compassion, creativity, and resilience—and, for me, too.

Would I do it again? In a heartbeat.

Which brings me to my new goal now that I've stepped back from the duties of day-to-day management. When I told Lee Keet that his $1 million matching grant offer was strategic and catalytic, he said, "That's exactly what I aspire to with my philanthropy." I will take the torch Lee passed and challenge others to think about what they want to do with their philanthropy.

I feel lucky to have the extra time to share All Hands' message of engagement and volunteerism. I believe so strongly in both. I'm eager to talk to people in the hope of leading them to experiment with that path in their own way.

Meanwhile, you're all welcome to join the Good (for Nothing) Club. The membership is free and the rewards are incalculable.

Project Nepal and the Future of All Hands Volunteers

Just before noon on April 25, 2015, the earthquake that scientists had been predicting (and dreading) for decades blasted Nepal. We knew immediately that this was a Big D—one of the biggest in years, in fact. We were ready—ready to go and ready to prove that we're a major player.

We announced to our volunteer community that we would be on site more quickly than we ever have in the past. And we got boots on the ground even faster than we'd planned. Our first assessment team of seven people arrived in the Nepalese capital of Kathmandu within seventy-two hours of the earthquake. As soon as cell phone service was restored, a few former All Hands volunteers had reached out to us, each one saying a variation on, "I'm in Kathmandu. Do you need my help?" A rapid response team mobilized and headed there immediately. Airbnb provided housing and the All Hands alumni in Nepal spread the word that we were coming on social networks, by posting signs in the streets and notifying guest houses and travelers' hostels. Within a week, thirty to forty people were showing up at our guest house/operations base every day, eager for our response team to put them to work in supply distribution and rubble removal.

During those first few weeks, we made the strategic decision to commit to a two-year project. That's the first time we have ever committed to a long-term stay so early in a disaster response. But it's consistent with our evolution from an organization that only executes disaster response to one that also provides long-term rebuilding and recovery. We have often said that our first five years prepared us for Haiti and our experience in Haiti prepared us for the next five years. Now, we found ourselves in Nepal, at our tenth-year anniversary, looking toward our next five years. In Haiti, we expanded our efforts into constructing biosand filters and building schools—critical pieces of the long view to recovery. Now we're fundamentally structured with the commitment to go into every situation thinking about the short-term response and also looking forward, asking, "Is there a need for us to do long-term recovery?"

Our long-term rebuild-and-recovery platform enhances our ability to respond to the immediate disaster. It provides space and time for staff to develop and grow and allows for a myriad of continuing opportunities for volunteers. It allows for All Hands to retain staff and institutional knowledge. We can be sustainable.

As a result, when a Big D, like the earthquake in Nepal occurs, we can quickly scale up.

We're moving aggressively in Nepal, and it's a good thing. We have one base in Kathmandu but our main base is in the Sindhupalchok district, where 88 percent of the population was displaced from their homes and is now living in displacement camps or in makeshift shelters typically constructed from tarps. More than two thousand people from eighty-three different countries applied to volunteer. We received applications from people in Chile, India, Finland, Iceland, Bulgaria, and Nigeria. We are now a vehicle for people from around the globe to help. That's a real affirmation of what we've already accomplished and what we hope to accomplish. While our response team has been removing rubble and clearing pathways to help pave the way for the urgently needed rebuild operations, the rebuild team has been initiating a reconstruction strategy focusing on housing and schools.

The FastTrack home building plan we are using in Nepal began with a conversation with Sherry-Lea Bloodworth, someone I had met in Biloxi when we were responding to Hurricane Katrina in 2005. Now the head of the American Institute of Architects (AIA) Foundation, she was interested in having her organization become more active in disaster response. She reached out to ARCASIA, a consortium of architects from nineteen countries in Southeast Asia, and SoNA, its Nepal chapter member, as well as Cameron Sinclair, a pioneer in bringing architectural solutions to humanitarian crises. Together, we assembled the FastTrack plan, an accelerated way to get people back into permanent housing while respecting their preferences and cultural norms, using local materials, and employing local workers. These are all tenets outlined in Sinclair's book, *Design Like You Give a Damn*, the Bible for architecture in the developing world. We hope to engage with SoNA for expertise in dealing with the government in the communities where we'll be working, layer in post-disaster housing expertise from Cameron and ARCASIA, and leverage AIA's connections. It's the most expedient way to execute a good solution.

Our build plan has enough meat and, between All Hands and our partners, we have enough street cred that the Clinton Global Initiative (CGI)—a collection of foundations, corporations, and individuals around the world who are interested in international issues—invited us to submit the proposal for funding. This is a resounding endorsement of all that All Hands has achieved in the past ten years. You don't approach CGI for funding; they approach you. The FastTrack plan has a $3 million price tag. We're hopeful that CGI members will fund it.

Our School Rebuild program leverages our successes in Haiti and the Philippines. Over 45,000 classrooms were destroyed in Nepal—a staggering number—leaving one million children with no safe place to learn. We have connected with Room to Read, a San Francisco-based nonprofit organization that partners with local communities throughout the developing world in order to improve literacy and gender equality in education in the developing world. They've been working in Nepal for fifteen years and have identified sixty-six schools in the Nuwakot District of central Nepal, just a few hours from Kathmandu, for first priority rebuilding.

This is the first time Room to Read has worked in a post-disaster situation. Because of the scale of the disaster and the immediacy of the need, they're very excited about working with us and we're excited to partner with them. We give them surge capacity to build many more schools much faster; their deep local ties will ensure we're using local labor and local materials to build culturally appropriate—and earthquake-resistant—buildings. We plan to make our assessments in August, spend September securing government approvals, use October to mobilize workers and material, and begin construction in November.

Our work in Nepal also represents a passing of the torch from me to Erik Dyson and to a new team and a new structure. It's bittersweet, but I know it's best for the organization to let other hands hold the reins. I want All Hands to outlive me and we will expand our capacity by not making it dependent on one or two individuals but on a learned set of skills. Our response to Nepal demonstrates that All Hands is now strong enough to survive and grow on its own.

So, what does this mean for All Hands going forward?

Through our innovative volunteer-led model, we continue to be a disrupter in the disaster response space. We're not a disrupter in the sense that we throw away existing models; instead, we fill a niche that other larger organizations can't or shouldn't. There are gaps that aren't met by the current paradigm, and we have proven that we can fill those gaps in a different way. We create opportunities for people who want to help after a disaster in a way that allows them to fit that experience to their life, not according to a strict model. If you can't drop everything, we have long-term projects that enable you to fit us into your schedule when it's convenient for you. If you want to stay in the US, you can, and if you want to travel across the world, we have international rebuilding projects, too. We've structured the organization to have ongoing domestic and international programs that address big and small events. Similarly, we're open to working with people at different stages and places in their lives who want to participate in the work we do.

We don't pretend to have all the solutions, but we've found that our efforts are critical to the long-term recovery of communities that have been shattered by natural disasters. We help them build a pathway back to normalcy. We're able to do it thanks to all of the hands— and hearts—that have made All Hands Volunteers what it is today: a cool, happy, and surprisingly effective disaster response organization.

The All Hands Magic

When volunteers have been on project for a while, sometimes they'll write a little thank-you note to the staff. For Stefanie Chang, an All Hands board member, one of the most memorable thank-you notes came from Steve Dunn, a volunteer on Project Léogane in Haiti.

Steve wrote that when growing up, he was always a little surly and bristled against authority. He didn't want to be that way but that was the way he reacted to the structures and institutions he found himself in. However, on an All Hands project, he discovered that he was able to be the best version of himself.

"The physical rubble we're pushing back and forth and the structures we were building, that's just the tip," Steve wrote, reflecting on All Hands projects. "The profound impact of the work is on the people, on both ends—the communities we help and the volunteers who help them."

What happens in the "real world" that makes people feel they can be their most productive, most positive, best version of themselves? What turns a do-good vacation into a life-changing experience? What makes people eager to shovel muck and run with a loaded wheelbarrow in tropical heat, hauling load after load after load? What's the secret ingredient that transforms even the most cynical volunteers into All Hands cheerleaders who come back again and again?

Let them explain in their own words.

....

Gay Campbell, volunteer on many All Hands projects

My favorite part of any project is helping people get their lives back together. They've been so traumatized and have lost so much, and we're doing a little bit to get them back in their home. It's encouraging to them and it's a wonderful feeling for us.

For me, working on anything that impacts children is so meaningful, whether it's rebuilding their home, providing a safe play space, helping with their schools, or making their environment safe. I have a photo from one of our projects in Haiti. Classes had started at one of the schools we built and a little girl came running in late. She was probably a new first-grader and was all dressed up, with white lace anklet socks and bows in her hair. She took one step to go into school then stopped in her tracks, and a huge smile spread across her face. She was so shocked and pleased to see an actual classroom with everyone sitting down. It was a wonderful moment.

....

....

**Stefanie Chang, volunteer in Biloxi and Indonesia;
former All Hands full-time staff member;
now All Hands board member**

I studied computer science and electrical engineering, and graduated from college at twenty, but I didn't see how all this supermicrodevice physics fit into the bigger world.

When a disaster happens, a different set of skills comes into play. After a disaster, what's most important? Food, shelter, water, livelihoods. These are really tangible. All Hands helps you see the connection between the work you're doing and its impact. You start with a pile of rubble, and, by evening, the rubble is cleared and is piled on the side of the road.

What I learned was not so much specific practical skills. I'm pretty embarrassed that I spent five years with All Hands and my knowledge of carpentry is pretty basic. But I learned a lot about the unconventional stuff—how to crash-land in any environment and get something going; how to look ahead and try to think things through in order to be really efficient with resources; how to do things as simply as possible so they work for larger numbers.

And I learned how to wake up every morning knowing that I'd spend my day doing meaningful work.

....

**Ian D'Arcy, volunteer in Peru, Indonesia,
and Bangladesh; All Hands board member and
founder and director of All Hands UK**

I think what appeals to me most about All Hands is that it's a complete win-win situation: the people we help need the help and get the help, and the people who do the helping get an experience they could never get anywhere else. There are no losers in this situation.

Another great thing is the immediacy and simplicity of what we do. Literally you—or anyone—can get on a plane tomorrow, meet people face-to-face in their time of greatest need, and put yourself in a position to change that. I didn't know that it was possible for any man in the street to give immediate help to someone who needed it. It was a complete revelation to me that was possible, and I love that.

One of the great things about All Hands is its agility and flexibility. The fact that it can operate on a level that appeals to people directly, which a larger, more structured organization can't do. There's a balance of compassion with pragmatic realism but with a focus on compassion.

I feel incredibly lucky. All Hands gives me the opportunity to give something back, and to give life a little more value and worth. It provides something I can't imagine I would get anywhere else.

....

Jo-Ann and David (now deceased) Driscoll, volunteers on nearly every All Hands project since Biloxi

The question always comes up: Why spend money to volunteer when we could just send money? On Project Sawit, I was talking to an English teacher in a tent school. She said she had been talking to mothers and students, and she said, "People are so thankful that you took the time to come here to show you care."

It was the same in Japan. I started talking to a Japanese woman as we were waiting for the overnight bus back to

Tokyo. She began crying as she said, "Thank you so much for coming to show you care." We were strangers, but it meant so much to her that we were there.

Things like that really strike home.

....

Sue Glassnor, volunteer in Biloxi, Indonesia, Haiti, Detroit, and dozens more

All Hands opened a whole new world for me. I never thought I would travel by myself to a country where I didn't know the language just because I knew that whatever needed to be done, I could do that when I got there. But I went—to Peru, Haiti, the Philippines—and had very rewarding experiences.

I like being able to go into a project knowing that I am going to help someone in their process of recovery. You don't really know what you're going to be doing until you get there but everything you do is so needed.

I like the fact that the majority of the money All Hands raises goes into the communities where we are. I've seen that firsthand, and that keeps me coming back—I *know* their fund-raising efforts truly go back into communities we work on.

I was shocked to find out that other volunteer opportunities charge you to go. I was flabbergasted. You miss a lot of great people who can't afford to pay $1,000 a week. Not charging a daily rate keeps a lot of people coming back.

When I first started, I was forty-eight. You don't have to be a youngster to volunteer. My philosophy is, if you want to volunteer, you will find a way to make it happen. I like to talk to people, so doing assessments is a perfect fit. I get to know the people and the jobs we do. I get to do what I love to do. I'll continue to do it as long as I'm able to.

....

....

Adam and Renée Haber, volunteers in Biloxi and Haiti (Adam) and in Cedar Rapids (Adam and Renée); Adam is now an All Hands board member

Most of us lead pretty orderly lives, so when you go through something that leaves chaos in its wake, it's uprooting. With All Hands, you get comfortable with chaos and then you learn to move through it. The truth is, any one of us who lives long enough will encounter something devastating—whether it's a natural disaster, an illness, someone's death, or a financial upheaval. Learning how to tolerate it and get through it is an amazing gift. That's what All Hands volunteers get: that sense of competence that you can function in the midst of chaos. There's no greater gift.

....

Tom Jardim, volunteer in Haiti; director of Project Léogane's school building program

I learned the extreme satisfaction of pushing yourself really, really hard, being really uncomfortable, and doing it for the right reason—to help people. It's made me think a lot about the career I'm going to have, what I do, and the things we take for granted. When I got home [from Haiti], I kept realizing, everything we have here is a luxury. You get in your car—luxury. You sit on the toilet—luxury. You turn on the water and drink from the faucet—luxury. To know that is definitely life-changing.

....

....

April and Michal Jelinek, volunteers on Project Gonaives (Michal), Project Sawit (April), and Project Léogane (both), where they met and became the first All Hands couple to marry

Michal: I especially like the idea that pretty much anyone can sign up: young people, old people, strong people, weak people, educated people, uneducated people, people with some disability. One guy was really fat, not healthy. He'd be really tired after an hour with a shovel or sledgehammer. So he sat down and helped with the kids. As long as there is a spot, anyone can sign up. This concept attracts the best people you could meet, and the variety of people brings a lot of energy. No one cares how much work you do, just that you make your full effort.

April: Another key factor is that the distance between us and the community is so small. When you work with local volunteers every day, swinging a sledgehammer and sweating with them, you develop friendships. We used the same tap-taps [the local transportation] as the local guys, not the white SUVs used by the big NGOs. You're so removed from the community in those SUVs. You don't know what people need and aren't able to build the trust you need to accomplish anything. That's a big difference from other organizations I'd worked with. With All Hands, we have friendships in the community. We didn't do something for Haitians. We did it for Jean-Marc, Emanuel, Pierre and César.

When I first came to All Hands, I literally did not how to hammer a nail. I'm a city girl. I can discuss philosophy until four in the morning but if you handed me a hammer, I'd look at you like, *what is this?* I learned how to sledgehammer in Indonesia. The guy who taught me patiently told me how to hold it, made sure I was doing it correctly, kept checking, and over the next couple days, came up to me and said, "You're doing it really well." That gives you a lot of confidence afterwards—knowing that you can take care of these basic things. When I came from Indonesia to Haiti, I had just turned twenty-five. My dad asked me what I'd like for my birthday. I said, "A sledgehammer."

I first heard about the earthquake in Haiti just before I left for Indonesia. I was watching the footage on TV of an excavator scooping bodies to go into a mass grave. I felt such complete powerlessness, that there was nothing I could do. Six months or a year later, when I was in Haiti, that memory came back and I realized, no, I was now there doing something. That realization got rid of a lot of that feeling of not being able to do something about things bigger than us. You can't fix the world, but you can find one guy who needs rubble cleared or a family that needs a water filter, and if you start small, you can have a huge impact, one person at a time.

....

Bruce Jones, volunteer on almost every All Hands project since Thailand

I introduced my younger son to All Hands. At the time, he was a young man in college and didn't know what direction to take. When I came home from Project Cagayan de Oro, I said, "I'll buy you a ticket to the Philippines because I know this experience will mean everything to you. You will find your passion and your place." I've seen it over the years—young people get there and stay there. It is so rewarding and so fulfilling. He has since come to work on Staten Island and did Long Beach with me and did Arkansas and Oklahoma.

I'm proud as hell to have introduced him to volunteering and, especially, the All Hands family.

Whenever I return home from a project, I talk to my church, to the Rotary Club, to schools. My message is: You can do this. Your life will be enriched when you come out of a project. It's about helping someone who needs it but that's not the end result.

Every year, I gain forty to fifty Facebook friends through All Hands. But every year, there's a handful that will become lifelong friends. I challenge anyone to tell me where you can meet fifty new friends every year and gain a handful of dear, lifelong friends. It's the situation, the place, the people—everything together.

The people you work for become family. There's no way you can achieve the relationships with local people when you go as a tourist. I become part of a community. I go to church with them and to their houses for Sunday meals. It's such a humbling experience for me. It keeps me grounded.

All Hands has made me a much better person. It's my reward for working hard all summer, knowing that in November, I'm going to a Hands project.

....

**Lee Keet, one of the original Super Friends;
volunteer in Peru; matching donor to Impact Fund**

Rewarding is the only word I can use. You're doing things for others with others. You immediately have a family in the other volunteers, you're all in it together, you've all made a sacrifice. It's heartwarming to see other people making sacrifices for other people, and it puts you into a fraternity of people whom you might not necessarily ever have picked out of a crowd to be friends with or to work with. Yet there's a sense of trust and camaraderie.

It's something our modern world actually discourages—this camaraderie, this team spirit, working together for a common purpose. When people—especially young people—have never seen it, it is life-changing. You discover you have to rely on other people and share experiences you would never get to share. It is certainly a very rewarding experience.

Meeting volunteers from all over the world will have lasting effects on the thousands of children touched by AHV.

Andrew Kerr, volunteer in Cedar Rapids; staffer until 2012

All Hands has this giant ripple effect. You can't put a value on it. It does incredible work helping people after a disaster and giving this experience to volunteers, but it also shifts people's lives—like Michal and April meeting and marrying. He's an acoustical engineer from Eastern Europe, and April was reading about string theory. They meet in Haiti and end up getting married. I went from a career in banking to nonprofits. My girlfriend is someone I met on an

All Hands project. A friend—I call her my second little sister—was a purchaser for Neiman Marcus but burned out on fashion, so she volunteered for ten days in Haiti. After she went home, she came back for another three months, then quit her job, got a degree in public health at Columbia University, and now works for a medical NGO in Sierra Leone. I don't know if that would have happened if she hadn't come to volunteer.

What I especially liked about All Hands is how integrated they get into the community. Working side by side with community members, bonding with community members—I haven't seen that with any other international aid organizations.

Among NGOs in Haiti, there's a joke that you're not a real NGO until there's a demonstration in front of your base. Whenever the population got mad at an NGO and felt they were treated unjustly, they'd block off the base with a wall of rocks and tires and set it on fire. That never happened to us, because we were so integrated in the community.

....

Neil Lawson, volunteer on twelve projects; met his wife, Jess Thompson, through All Hands

I have completely changed because of All Hands. I went to Peru because I had the idea that I would become a social worker and I wanted to learn more Spanish. The only way I could pay for it was by joining a volunteer group.

When I joined All Hands, it was the first time in my life where I did any manual labor. Even just shoveling debris, I'd never done it before. It kicked my ass. But I became stronger and more physically able to do things. And from there, I kept doing different sorts of All Hands projects. I worked on rubble and salvage projects in Indonesia. I cleared drainage canals in Japan so people could get water flowing back into their homes.

From taking things apart and putting them together, you begin to see how things are made. Today, I have my own handyman business. I would never have done that if I hadn't started with All Hands. Everything I learned to do in construction comes from All Hands.

All Hands Volunteers is an unreal organization. It is not without its faults, but I truly believe no group on earth is as efficient and badass. It does things that no other disaster groups would ever think to do. The group has done everything from clearing out a hospital full of mud in the time of a cholera epidemic so people could be treated in it again, to clearing out fish factories after the Japan tsunami when the rotted fish smell crippled the town we lived in. All Hands is often the only group that offers on-site cleanup and rebuild support on lesser-known disasters. Without them, there would be people who could never get the help they need.

In many ways, All Hands made me understand myself more than anything else that has happened to me before or after. That's why I have made All Hands the most constant endeavor in my life.

....

Diana Manilla, volunteer on Project Léogane; managed the cash-for-work and biosand filter programs

I have never seen another volunteer organization that allows its volunteers to interact with the community as much as All Hands does. I observed how many volunteers built really meaningful bonds with local community members and how that created a great acceptance of All Hands volunteers in the community, and I have yet to see anything like that with other aid organizations.

....

Becci Manson. volunteer on Project Tohoku, where she spearheaded the photo restoration project

You have moments when you have these ideas or thoughts, and you can choose to follow through or put them in the back of your mind and forget about them. Most of my life, I'd done the latter. But to see what we could do in six months, from absolute inception to finish—and do it with the encouragement of a lot of people—was an amazing experience. For me, it was, *this* is what happens when I don't walk away from one of my ideas.

I'm still trying to follow up on that through the TED Talk, speaking at SXSW, talking in schools. I've always been incredibly shy, so that's made a huge difference—to do something every day that scares you, and do it again and again. It's not so difficult for me now.

My partner said, "Even if you don't do other things, you've inspired a lot of people." And that's true. A kid on one of the Hurricane Sandy projects said, "You've inspired me. I'm writing a thesis about how creative people can help in a disaster. Your TED Talk is the perfect example."

A friend told me something many years ago: People will trust me now when I do have the thought. It's not just someone making noise with no follow-up. The most important thing is that I believe in myself a little more. If I do follow through on an idea, what's the worst thing that can happen?

....

Nick Taranto, volunteer in Biloxi, Indonesia, and Haiti; current All Hands board member

I first met the organization when I was nineteen and went to Thailand after the tsunami, then I joined Project Sawit after I graduated from college. I had volunteered for soup kitchens in the US, but I had never done anything like that internationally. It was a way to get into the lives of people whom I would never have met and see them at their most raw and vulnerable and be there to help. That exposure as a young person is really crucial, as is the experience of seeing how someone else lives and suffers, especially if you're from the US. I returned thinking that our cars are so big and our sodas so large and we take so much for granted. I wish more people had that exposure. It puts everything in perspective.

I took a group of thirty-five Dartmouth students to volunteer in Biloxi. A lot of us had never been in an environment like that before. If you grew up on the Upper East Side of New York and went to an Ivy League school and now you're in hurricane-ravaged Mississippi using a chainsaw, that's a pretty different experience to have. There are an infinite number of stories like that among All Hands volunteers. You're put in challenging positions with people whom you just would not interact with on a regular basis, and that's why people come to love All Hands.

It can be a profound experience to work on something bigger than yourself with people who are there not for financial aim or because it's the cool thing to do or because it looks good on a resume, but because it feels right. You go through these experiences that are novel and scary. They really sear themselves into you. So even though you can only volunteer for a week or a day, I think it's something we need more of.

....

Jess Thompson, volunteer on Project Sawit; current All Hands volunteer coordinator

The fact that they don't charge is a big thing—that my work was so valuable to them that they would host me for free. As a long-term traveler without much money, it allowed me to stay much longer and get a much richer experience.

I've never seen people work so hard, so long for no financial reward. I think there's a different relationship between the volunteer and the project if there is a fee involved. If I had paid for my food and accommodations and I was tired when I woke up one morning, I might stay in bed and not go into the field, because I've covered my costs already. Whereas this way, there is that gratitude from the All Hands population that enabled me to come and do this amazing work and help this community when they needed it, so my work is an exchange for all the logistics the community put in place.

You're working side by side with members of the community. And it's physical work that comes with an entirely different satisfaction level than the kind of work you do at home, where you don't see the tangible results of your work. At the end of the day, you see with your eyes what you've achieved—and it's not a gray area. You've helped someone do something.

A repeat volunteer once told me that there are two kinds of people in this world: the people who run with wheelbarrows and the people who ask why. The reason you run with the wheelbarrow is because the person will get their house back sooner. It's hard and hot and intense, but you don't ask why, you just keep on doing it.

With All Hands, I knew I had found something wonderful and I couldn't imagine doing anything else. It's been so life-changing for so many of us that we want to make sure it's the same for the next people who come through.

....

Marc Young, volunteer in Biloxi and key staffer for eight years

It's very addicting to be useful. You're overwhelmingly compelled every day to work as hard as you can physically in order to get done as much as you can get done that day—and then repeat and then repeat. The reward and satisfaction that comes from that effort allows you to continue.

From a life standpoint, it's changed me. The life-changing part was discovering a willingness to drop everything and go help. And now I know that I should, because I can have an impact. One person *can* make a difference. I can't imagine myself doing anything else.

Nancy and Becca are all hands with the tots.

....

A Day in the Life of a Volunteer

Hard, manual labor is a given on every All Hands project. But the effort pays off with a surprising bonus: not just how your work resonates throughout the community but also how surprisingly enjoyable it can be to spend hours mucking, gutting, sledgehammering, and sweating, with some of the most interesting people you'll ever meet.

Arrival

Most new arrivals get their first real introduction to All Hands at the 5:00 p.m. nightly meeting, a deep dive into logistics that epitomizes the special combination of practicalities and purpose that defines All Hands.

The meeting begins with a welcome for the new volunteers.

"They do this really well. It's a way to make new people feel they're involved in the community from the beginning. You feel the rush immediately that you're part of something big."

—Renee Haber

"If you've just arrived, you're asked to introduce yourself: who you are, where you're from, how long you're planning to stay, how you heard about All Hands. And then you're asked some off-the-wall question, like, 'What was the greatest invention of all time?' or 'What was greatest gift you ever received?' or 'If you were a super-hero, who would you be?'"

—Sue Glassnor

"I was asked, 'If you were a Disney character, which one would you want to be?' I have daughters, so I see a lot of the princess movies. But I didn't think it was appropriate to talk about princesses, so I said I'd be Goofy."

—Erik Dyson

Then the topic moves on to a recap of the different jobs done throughout the day—who dug this trench and who built that fence. Everyone is invited to speak up. You might get some funny stories, and you might hear how homeowners have reacted. You'll hear about the things that go right and wrong in the process.

"After the different housekeeping items, they talk about the work planned for the next day—gutting this house, installing sanitation at that house, rebuilding somewhere else, cleaning cages at the animal shelter. You might not like to do one thing so you can look into doing another job that might interest you more. You get the opportunity to experience everything when you're there."

—Sue Glassnor

"People who are first responders are trained to deal with disasters. You're coming in as second responder, but seeing the devastation is very emotional and overwhelming. The nightly meetings are an opportunity to let some of that emotion out. It helps people process what they're going through. Even if you're not saying anything, someone else is probably saying what you feel."

—Renee Haber

To close the meeting, volunteers who are leaving are invited to stand up and say good-bye.

"It's very emotional. People choke up. You see that pure, unadulterated experience. Even if you've just arrived and never met that person who's leaving, you can't help but think, 'Wow, that was an amazing experience.' You can't help but think about what you're going to say when it's time for you to leave. It forces self-introspection right from the beginning, which is pretty amazing."

—Erik Dyson

Everyone—even experienced staffers—benefits from the nightly meetings.

Living in the communities that we are helping gives us a better awareness of their realities.

"As a director/coordinator, I'm in the office, trying to get the larger structures in place. I'm not the one shoveling rubble or interacting with community or playing with kids. The daily meeting reminds me how fresh, energetic, and tentative people are when they come in, and how profound and open and honest they are when they leave. It's a daily reminder of the privilege that we come from that allows us to do something like this."

—Stefanie Chang

"Those nightly meetings are just as important as sharing dinner. Dinner is nutritionally important—you've worked hard all day and need to replenish. The nightly meetings are emotionally nourishing."

—Renee Haber

Settling In

"It's like sleep-away camp" is the most common description—and not a particularly cushy camp, either. But, like the nightly meetings, the basic living conditions are a key part of the All Hands culture.

"Conditions can be very crowded. A lot of people who work on these projects are young and used to communal living. They're not that far away from college dorm life or having six people in a house. For older people, going back to communal living is definitely more of a challenge. But we've met some fantastic people, so that helps make it a positive experience. And for the most part, people are very accommodating, considering how little personal space you have."

—Joanne Driscoll

"In Haiti, the base was located in an old dance club next to Joe's Bar. It was very rudimentary: bucket showers, wood planking for bunk beds with mosquito nets, a couple of unshaded light bulbs, peanut butter and banana and bread for breakfast. But after you see how the locals are living, having electricity and a bucket shower was a luxury."

—Nick Taranto

"Marc [Young] was originally in charge of making breakfast, but he had to go somewhere, so I said I could do it. Making breakfast means waking up at 5:00 a.m., making coffee, and preparing some cereal, bread and peanut butter. Another guy had put up a small board advertising Ribaud Coffee. I started to change the names: Mud Coffee, Black Night Coffee, or if someone was leaving, I named a coffee after him. We had a crazy rooster next door that was being raised for cockfighting, so we had Crazy Rooster Morning Coffee."

—Michal Jelinek

"In Indonesia, there was only one bathroom, so we sometimes ducked out into the rainforest because there could be quite a queue in the morning. The showers were a curtain and a five-gallon bucket of water, but when it's hot and sticky, you don't mind. You're happy to be clean for just a little bit. We took rain showers, too. If it rained at the right time, you could step out and use the rain to wash your hair. In Haiti, the water ran off the roof in streams. You'd see a bunch of people run out in their bathing suits or underwear and shower right there."

—April Jelinek

"Some people might not like sleeping with fifty people you don't know in the same room. In one place, all the snorers had to sleep on one side. Earplugs are a good thing. Always bring extra earplugs."

—Sue Glassnor

"I heard more complaints about snoring in the guys' quarters than we had."

—April Jelinek

"Is it uncomfortable? Oh, yeah. You're always hot and sticky. It's either hot or hotter. You exit the shower and you're drying yourself off. Then, at some point, the water turns into sweat. I had mosquito bites all over, all the time. You couldn't let your skin be without a blanket of mosquito spray unless you were under a mosquito net. When I'm home, one of the things I realize is that I can take a shower and *not* put on mosquito spray. I slept on a plywood bunk-bed with a one-inch pad for eight months. But I got used to the discomfort. It wasn't the defining characteristic of my life in Haiti."

—Tom Jardim

"In Haiti, after dark, the base was locked down for safety. You felt a bit like you were in a war zone sometimes. But All Hands does an amazing job of maintaining security and making people feel safe in situations that could be intimidating."

—Nick Taranto

"I was in Haiti when they were having the elections. Haitians call them *manifestation*s; I call them riots. To keep the volunteers safe, our base was on lockdown for four days. To release monotony, we came up with the 'Lockdown Olympics.' There were relay races and tightrope walking. You had to run backwards to a certain point, tag another team member, and they had to skip or hop to another point. As part of the relay race, your team would go to all these different areas on the base and perform a task. At one area, you had to talk to someone in Mandarin and see if the person could actually understand you."

—Sue Glassnor

"I felt safe in the camp. We were in a secure building, but we were surrounded by a tent city of displaced persons. I loved sitting on the roof and listening to the people sing. They had nothing, but they sang spirituals every night. It was unbelievable sitting up there at night, listening to them sing. That was my reward for the day."

—Bruce Jones

The All Hands Diet

"I'm not very fussy about my food. I can eat the same thing over and over again," said Jo-Ann Driscoll, who has volunteered in Biloxi, Indonesia, Peru, Haiti, Japan, Bangladesh, and the Philippines. That's good, because, she continued, "The food is . . . well, something you must get used to."

"In most places, you can generally get to a village and find something you like. Except in Bangladesh—we all lost weight on that one. We brought protein bars with us, so we could supplement our diet. Sometimes we'd request things, like hard-boiled eggs, and that would give us the protein we needed."

—Jo-Ann Driscoll

"You don't have to eat rice and beans with a fish head for too many meals to get tired of it. David asked me what my highest recommendation would be when I was leaving. Because I'm on the board, I knew the food budget per day per volunteer was $1.73. I said, 'We can go to $2 per day. Let's get a little more chicken into the rice.'"

—Mike McQueeney

Off to Work

Although All Hands is best known for its work in mucking and gutting, you never know what tasks might arise or what opportunities might present themselves. What you *do* know is that you'll work hard—and have fun doing it.

"As you walk down the street in the All Hands Volunteers T-shirt, people might not know your name but they know you're a volunteer and they provide the same friendliness and welcome. When you first arrive in what you may think of as a scary place, and then you find people who are welcoming and wave and say hello, that's motivating."

—Stefanie Chang

"When you show up on a location, there's usually a project manager. He or she could be someone who's been there just a week more than you but knows a bit more. You're given tasks that are mostly semiskilled labor—mixing concrete, plastering, window framing. They'll teach you the technique they're using. It's not difficult work and you learn as you go. I didn't know how to mix concrete before I went, but I can now mix concrete with the best of them. You know your concrete is going to last a generation and you want it to withstand the next earthquake, so you feel a responsibility to do it right."

—Adam Haber

"What's unbelievable about the organization is the way they train people in real time. Whether you're gutting a house or working on mold remediation, after you've been there a week or two, regardless of age or background, you could be running a crew."

—Mike McQueeney

"The guy who taught me to sledgehammer in Indonesia was really efficient. I said, 'I'd like to try but I don't even know how to hold it.' He patiently told me how to hold it, made sure I was doing it correctly, and kept checking on me over the next couple days. Then one day, he came up to me and said, 'You're doing it really well.'

One of the best All Hands stories was about a girl from South Korea who didn't know how hold a hammer when she came to Haiti. She learned carpentry on the project and ended up building beautiful furniture."

—**April Jelinek**

"Hee, a young woman from South Korea, had never had any experience in and didn't have the confidence to sign up for construction. I was leading a crew doing school building and I said, 'Just sign up on my team.' We were studding up the walls and she said, 'I can't do that.' I taught her how to swing a hammer and hit a nail. Then we got into roofing and putting trusses together. She said, 'I want to get up there.' I said, 'Whenever you're ready.' By the end of one or two schools, Hee was on the roof doing everything everyone else did. When I left, she knew what was right and what was wrong, and if she saw someone doing something wrong, she was first to say, 'Bruce would not let you do it this way.'"

—**Bruce Jones**

"There's always music on the job site and a fun atmosphere. If you're too strict because you think people are goofing off, that's not going to be productive. People need to get a good vibe. We had boom boxes throughout the project in Haiti. Definitely some *konpa* was being played. Valsin, a Haitian volunteer who became a paid construction worker, was a tough character. But I always think of him dancing while he walked from one side of the job site to another."

—**Tom Jardim**

"We would work from 7:30 a.m. to 11:30 a.m. and then have lunch. In that heat, it took everything you had just to get to lunch. There'd be a ninety-minute break and you'd find a cool piece of cement and lie down, so you could find enough energy to get out there and do it again. You play mind games to help people get through the day. We'd sing songs, list the seven wonders of the world, and ask people to describe the highest place they'd ever been."

—Bruce Jones

"I've worked on four projects and come into contact with hundreds of volunteers. They all shared a similar personality trait: They were gung ho. I'd wake up dead tired and they'd be saying, 'Let's do it again!' Even in Haiti, where it was so hot, and you could still feel the tremors of the aftershocks, and the dogs were barking all night, and you were eating rice and beans day after day, they never got burned out. They were there for adventure and purpose, and they all worked hard."

—Adam Haber

"When I first got to Léogane, it was incredibly hot and we went to break up concrete slabs and wheelbarrow out the rubble. The team leader suggested we get a partner and do ten and ten: one person takes ten blows with the sledgehammer, then hands it off to their partner and rests while the partner swings ten times. I partnered with a young woman, a teacher from New York City. She couldn't have weighed more than 115 pounds but she was swinging away. On my fifth swing, I was gasping for air. I said, 'If you don't mind, you and I will do ten and five, and the five I do will take as long as ten, so you'll get some rest.'

I was very impressed by what people put into it. I didn't see any slacking in these volunteers. Their belief was, 'I left my home and comfort to come here. It would be pointless to sit around and goof off because it's not a vacation spot.' Every volunteer I knew was a hard worker."

—Jack Ferrebee

"One of the great things about All Hands is the agility, the flexibility, and the freedom—you can choose the project you want to work on. If you meet people on the street and you have an idea for a project while you're serving, then people will listen to you and you can carry out that project."

—Ian D'Arcy

"In Java, most of the community was covered in tarps. But what these folks needed was not another roof, because roofs would come eventually, but a way to get back on their feet. I teamed up with a bunch of local guys who had been democracy advocates to do microlending. All Hands got the seed funding to enable us to give small loans—about $65 on average—so people could start generating money again.

We had trainers who sat down with people before they got their loan to explain how it worked. The community was so tight-knit that when someone couldn't repay the loan, others would help. They'd rather help their neighbor than have him default.

Our loans helped one person fix a cart from which he sold fried tofu on the street. Another family was able to buy a brick-making machine and created bricks that All Hands and others in the community bought and used to build houses. Microlending wasn't in a typical All Hands capacity, but they saw the community needed this and were able to catalyze it."

—Nick Taranto

"You declare what you want to do and what you don't want to do and you end up with that job. That's why it's so soul-satisfying. If you don't want to use a chainsaw, you can be a cook, and if you don't know how to cook, you can be a cook's helper or wash dishes.

It takes ingenuity and smarts to be a really effective volunteer. Of course, there's grunt work—the scullery maid and garbage guy don't have to be rocket scientists. But most people need ingenuity, independence, and self-confidence. Those are the three critical components. And most people are pretty ingenious and creative."

—Lee Keet

"If someone had a suggestion to help the community, no matter what it was, I rarely heard someone say, 'We can't do that.' If it sounded like something that needed to be done, our project director would try to do it. We had volunteers who were engineers and architects and would come up with inventive ideas.

One of our engineers knew about biosand filters. You could purify water with gravel and sand and micro-organisms that grow in the top layer of sand. It's very simple. For $100, the cost of the materials, one biosand filter could purify water for a family of four for ten years. Just amazing. And one of our volunteers came up with that."

—Jack Ferrebee

"Making the biosand filters was a tedious process. You put the sand in and pounded it down but if you didn't do it right, it wouldn't do what it was meant to do. After volunteering with the group building the filters, I helped when they were being installed and saw how they actually worked. Seeing the whole process from start to finish was really neat."

—Sue Glassnor

"We had a problem with the biosand filters. We spent hours and hours washing and sifting the sand. Then Michal had the idea of rigging a bicycle to the sand sifter. People shoveled sand into the sifter and you got on the bike and pedaled. It was the coolest."

—April Jelinek

"There are different opportunities every day. In Haiti, we were building schools, making compostable toilets, and making water filters. They'd come up with the neatest projects."

—Sue Glassnor

"A Haitian-run hospital in Léogane had flooded during the hurricane. It was filled with mud about one meter deep. The people at the hospital were looking at it as a loss, but we said, 'We can do this.' We brought a team in for a two-week project. We built these huge mops by nailing together two-by-fours, ripping up foam sleeping pads, and stapling them on the bottom of the two-by-fours. We lined up in two rows with our mops. The coordinator stood at one end of the hall and shouted, 'Go!' and we'd run down the hall and try to push the mud out the door. It was a fun project."

—April Jelinek

"The workers at the orphanages were overwhelmed by the number of children, so we'd go there and play with the kids. We had jump ropes and balls and chalk. At one point, All Hands volunteers created a dance and the kids performed it. They loved it—they always wanted to do the dance."

—Sue Glassnor

"The little kids always want to help, so we almost always appoint one volunteer as a kid wrangler to take care of all the kids who gather around and keep them safe and occupied. Some volunteers bring Frisbees on a project. I'll do an art project with them. When we're finished building a school or a playground, the kids help paint it. We often have the kids dip their hands in blue paint and put their imprint on the project."

—Gay Campbell

Volunteer shows joy over the AHV experience and anguish
at leaving during her last nightly meeting.

Everyone is Welcome

One of the attractions of All Hands is that it's "age- and sex-neutral," said Gay Campbell. "There is no bias toward any volunteer who comes."

"I get as many questions from eighteen-year-olds asking whether they will be the youngest person on the project as from fifty-year-olds asking if they will be the oldest. There are always questions about fitting in. But I always say that the beauty of All Hands is that everyone gives 110 percent of what they've got, not 110 percent of the guy next to you. As long as you give your all, nobody will criticize you. When we're sledgehammering concrete, someone needs to shovel it into a wheelbarrow—that's a much less intense task. In Indonesia, we were pulling nails out of wood and chipping mortar off bricks so families could reuse them. There was something for everyone to do on that site."

—Jess Thompson

"I was forty-eight when I first started with All Hands. You don't have to be a youngster to volunteer. Young or old, it seems like 99.9 percent of the time, everyone gets along. You make friends quickly, and I have quite a few lasting relationships from the people I've met. Some are my kids' age. Age doesn't really play into it. You just form a camaraderie. You have more in common than you think."

—Sue Glassnor

"I have had wonderful young architects show me how to take measurements for a building. The stronger volunteers don't grab tools out of your hand; they show you how to use them properly. I also know how to hand-make concrete, because I did that for a floor in Peru. I've learned so many skills."

—Gay Campbell

"It's true that a lot of what we do is very physical. I love to gut buildings—it's one of my favorite things to do. There's a feeling of satisfaction that you're getting this thing ready to get to the next phase of recuperation. Gutting a house doesn't have to be physical, though. Sometimes it involves carrying trash outside, not taking a sledgehammer and going at a wall.

A lot of projects aren't as physical as they sound. In Biloxi, we were working with the Salvation Army to hand out food and toilet paper or walking dogs at local shelter because no one was left to do that. In Haiti, we had the biosand filter project and some people got into business-building. In Bangladesh, we put up schools but it wasn't heavy, heavy work because of the nature of the building. You held up woven fiber mats so someone could hammer them into the posts."

—Jo-Ann Driscoll

Gay teaches English next to a new school build project.

"It's sexy and cool to show a young lady swinging a sledgehammer. But there are thousands of jobs that people can do that are important to the community and you don't have to be a buff twenty-two-year-old to do them. If you need to take a break every fifteen minutes, no one will harass you so long as you're working hard. It's not like you won't get dinner if don't carry a hundred-pound bag of cement.

In the Philippines, after Typhoon Haiyan, we had a fifty-year-old volunteer from Brazil who had never traveled outside of his native country. He got on a plane, came to Tacloban, and then said to the team, 'You need someone to clean up the base. I'll do that job.' He spent every day cleaning the toilets and sweeping. He decided that, for him, it was the most rewarding part. He had great relationships with the volunteers, because they were happy he was there."

—Erik Dyson

Day-trippers

"Not everyone has ability to travel overseas and stay for a long time," explained Jess Thompson, the All Hands volunteer coordinator. "Day volunteers often live in the area and come to volunteer because something happened in their area. That can be a different type of person and at different stage of life. But that doesn't change their commitment to the project, because local people have a big commitment to fix their community."

"I met David Campbell in 2012 and subsequently I've worked on three Superstorm Sandy-related projects. I'd love to do longer-term work, but I need to figure out how and when. Meanwhile, I see my role as not just about me going out and doing a day's worth of work but working on a broader agenda: trying to build the partnership with Credit Suisse—I'm a managing director in the information technology group—and All Hands. I've been an internal advocate to promote more corporate giving and to get the Credit Suisse Foundation to view All Hands as a marquee group we want to support.

After Sandy hit, local disaster organizations were collecting stuff at my neighborhood local park. Everyone came out to help but there was not a lot of organization and the aid wasn't impactful and productive.

I used Project Staten Island as an opportunity to bring together a team of thirty volunteers from Credit Suisse. (We later had Credit Suisse teams volunteer for a day on Project Long Island and

Project Brooklyn.) With All Hands, there's a structure, site leaders, tasks to be done and specific duties. The feeling is, you're going to be there for a day, so let's get done what we can do.

All Hands gave us a steer on what to wear and what to bring: work clothes and boots, work gloves. When we got to the site, they provided us with ventilators and gloves for people who didn't have them, and they had all the tools. There was a quick demo on "here's the easiest way to get the floor tiles up or pull the drywall down." You watch other people doing it and follow the leader. There's always a supervisor who works with you and your team.

We divided into three teams of ten and there was competition: Who was going to gut the most homes and make the most impact for these affected families? You feel you're truly making a difference because of the people they partner you with and the tools and resources they give you.

At the end of the day, everyone felt very satisfied. They felt proud to be a part of it and were grateful that they were able to help. They felt they had done a good day's work and a good deed. There was a universal positive vibe and a sentiment that they wanted to do more. As a result, when we did Project Brooklyn this last time, we had to shut down the booking because there were more volunteers than even All Hands could handle for a day."

—Greg Dietrich

The Unexpected Bonus

When volunteers look back on their All Hands experiences, one of the most common sentiments is their surprise at the people they meet on project, both among their fellow volunteers and the local community. Deep friendships regularly spring up. And sometimes they turn into something more. "Neil [Lawson] and I are the fifth couple to meet and marry because of All Hands," said Jess Thompson. "There have been two more since then, so All Hands is responsible for seven marriages altogether."

"You seem to have more in common with these people because they chose to do what you chose to do. I've made so many lifelong friendships, because 98 percent of people who come to All Hands just 'get it.' You're all there for the same reasons."

—Jess Thompson

"In Biloxi, I was on the termite crew. My partner was a young woman and we worked together all day, dragging branches out to the street after the chainsaw gang cut them into a manageable size. Back at the base that evening, she told me her story. She is a molecular biologist. She had planned to spend her vacation time painting her living room. She had bought all the paint and been about to open the first can when she realized, 'There are people who don't even have walls to paint,' and came to volunteer. It doesn't matter what you do in your regular life. You can still help."

—Gay Campbell

"I was particularly impressed by the young people who volunteered. At one of the nightly meetings, someone suggested that it was a great thing that older volunteers would come down to Haiti. I said, 'That's entirely backward. We have nothing but free time on our hands and our careers are behind us. These young folks coming here are giving up a lot.' I was much more impressed by what nineteen-, twenty- and twenty-one-year-olds were willing to do to be able to volunteer. Some would have to go home periodically to work to have enough money to afford to come back."

—Jack Ferrebee

"In the very early days after the Haiti earthquake, I was walking down the street with a young woman volunteer who was born in Haiti, grew up in New York City, and was now successful in the finance industry in South Africa. An elderly gentleman approached us and said he had lost everything and could we please help him. The volunteer said, 'We have all left our jobs and families and homes to come and help you. We don't have anything to give except ourselves.' The man said, 'Well, then I should be helping you.' And the next day, while we were clearing rubble from a home, this man appeared with his nephew and proceeded to send his nephew up a tree to cut down coconuts. He showed us how to drink the juice and eat the flesh and explained how in that climate coconuts were the best thing to restore our energy. We had the best time with that man and his nephew, and we were very much restored."

—Gay Campbell

"On the anniversary of the Haiti earthquake, we gathered that evening with the locals, and they told stories of where they were when the earthquake hit. They were all terrible stories, all personal tragedies of how they lost someone. My heart broke listening to them. I learned how people can go through total disaster, their lives collapsed, everything gone. But then you see a year later how they've moved on, how they can work again, how things are changing. Their stories sounded like the end of the world. But those people survived and are fine now, and our organization helped."

—Michal Jelinek

"My favorite part of a project is sitting down for dinner with eight to ten volunteers and asking, 'How did you get here?' It's amazing to me that there's never a consistent journey. It's not like everyone graduated from college and was looking for something to fill the three months before grad school. Especially on international projects, they're literally from all over the world, every corner. They have different accents. They're twenty-two, thirty-two, forty-two, fifty-two years old. They have amazing qualifications yet are there just to do good. There's no hidden agenda like, 'I'm here to get into business school' or "My mother made me come.'

On every project, whether it's in Detroit or the Philippines, I see the passion, energy, commitment, and desire to do good. It's really inspirational. Last year, I took my daughter to the Philippines, and my wife and I went on a few projects. We always think, 'These are the coolest people I've ever met and I never would have met them if I hadn't been here.' You meet amazing people who've had amazing life journeys, and they're doing great things for the world. It gives you a sense of hope and a sense of promise."

—Erik Dyson

ALL of our volunteers are GIANTS, as shown by Marine Matt!

What's In Your Go-bag?

"When you're on project, you have your bunk space and that's it," warns All Hands board member and long-time volunteer Ian D'Arcy. There's no space for excess gear.

When you sign up for a trip, you'll receive a list of suggested items to bring with you. In addition, the volunteers interviewed for this book offered their own suggestions for making life pleasant on project. What constitutes a necessity—or even a "nice-to-have"—varies from volunteer to volunteer and from project to project. Will you be volunteering on an international project or a domestic one? Will you sign up for a multiday stay or be a day-tripper? In all cases, whether you're traveling with a duffel bag or a daypack, save room to stuff in your sense of humor.

Clothing

- Wrinkle-free pants

  "As you move from field to board-room style meetings, you'll need to dress appropriately. You can get away with a T-shirt—it's like wearing muddy boots, it gives credibility. But you need decent wrinkle-free pants. You can sleep in them, just roll out of bed and go to a meeting."

  —Bill Driscoll

- Long-sleeved shirts and long pants

  "Even though the temperature is in high nineties and the humidity is ninety percent, as a woman, I might have to wear them because it's appropriate to the culture."

  —Jo-Ann Driscoll

  "Plus, they repel mosquitoes."

  —Gay Campbell

- Boots with puncture-resistant soles. No sneakers
- Good, cheap raingear

  "Anything you bring will get filthy."

  —Jo-Ann Driscoll

- Socks

  "Lots of socks. I can't stand for my feet to sweat all day and then put on a dirty pair of socks the next day."

  —Sue Glassnor

- Scarf or kerchief

  "You can wrap it around your nose and mouth to keep the dust out. And you can use it as a towel."

  —Gay Campbell

- One nice outfit or collared shirt

  "For going to the market or when you're invited to a community event. It's a respect thing."

  —Stefanie Chang

Food

- Vitamin pills to supplement your diet
- PowerBars or energy bars

  "You never know what the food is going to be like."   —Renee Haber

- Tea

  "It was so wonderful to have a cup of green tea at the end of a long day."

  —Diana Manilla

Gear

- Work gloves
- Headlamp

  "It's especially good when you go to the loo at night and might find a spider on the seat."   —Diana Manilla

- Swiss Army Knife or multi-tool

Personal Comfort

- Air mattresses

  "Sometimes the bunk beds have mattresses and sometimes they don't."

  —Jo-Ann Driscoll

- Inflatable pillow
- Fleece blanket
- Sleep sack or sheet
- Baby wipes

  "Within a day, you're covered in muck and a bucket shower never keeps you clean. A baby wipe ensures some semblance of being sanitary after you use the toilet. Get the wipes with major mosquito repellent."   —Adam Haber

- Mosquito net
- Bungee cords or twine

  "You can use it to hang the mosquito netting and also use it for a laundry line." **—Jo-Ann Driscoll**

- Earplugs or iPod loaded with audio books and/or sleep-inducing sounds

  "To block out the sounds of insects and snoring." **—Nick Taranto**

Spiritual Sustenance

- A good book

  "You need to take a break to get away from the project. I recommend *Any Human Heart* by William Boyd and *A Short History of Nearly Everything* by Bill Bryson." **—Ian D'Arcy**

Extras

- Gifts for locals

  "For Project Tohoku, I brought Boston Red Sox caps because we knew the Japanese love baseball and one of the pitchers for the Red Sox is Japanese." **—Stefanie Chang**

- Snacks and treats for other volunteers

  "Starbursts and Skittles—something sweet and a little chewy." **—Andrew Kerr**

  "Packages of different cooking spices in a foil pouch. After six weeks of Indonesian food, they're a completely different taste." **—Jess Thompson**

"Lifesavers." **—Gay Campbell**

"Peanut butter." **—Stefanie Chang**

- Travel guide

  "Try to learn a bit about the place, even if you're using the Lonely Planet series as a basic cultural guide, because that's important when meeting locals."

  —Stefanie Chang

APPENDIX 4

All Hands Current and Past Projects

International Projects:

01. 2004 HandsOnThailand, Bang Tao, Thailand, Tsunami

03. 2006 Project Yogjakarta, Sawit, Indonesia, Earthquake

04. 2006 Project Santo Domingo, Philippines, Typhoon

05. 2007 Project Pisco, Peru, Earthquake

06. 2007 Project Rayenda, Bangladesh, Cyclone

10. 2008 Project Gonaives, Haiti, Hurricane

13. 2009 Project Sungai Geringging, Indonesia, Earthquake

18. 2010-2012 Project Leogane, Haiti, Earthquake

24. 2011 Project Tohoku, Japan, Tsunami

25. 2012 Project Cagayan de Oro, Philippines, Typhoon

31. 2013 Project Pagatpat Rebuild, Philippines, Typhoon

37. 2013 Project Bohol Response, Philippines, Earthquake

38. 2013 Project Leyte Response, Philippines, Typhoon

41. 2014 Project Leyte Rebuild, Philippines, Typhoon

46. 2015 Project Samar Response, Typhoon

48. 2015 Project Malawi Response, Flooding

50. 2015 Project Samar Rebuild, Philippines, Typhoon

52. 2015 Project Nepal Response, Kathmandu, Earthquake

55. 2015 Project Nepal Response, Sindhpalchok, Earthquake

56. 2015 Project Malawi Rebuild, Flooding

Domestic Projects:

02. 2005 HandsOnUSA, Biloxi, Mississippi, Hurricane Katrina

07. 2008 Project Gassville, AR, Tornado

08. 2008 Project Newton County, Missouri, Tornado

09. 2008 Project Cedar Rapids, Iowa, Flooding

11. 2009 Project Mena, AR, Tornado

12. 2009 Project Gowanda, New York, Flooding

14. 2010 Project Cedar Rapids Rebuild, Flooding

15. 2010 Project Rhode Island, Flooding

16. 2010 Project Tennessee, Flooding

17. 2010 Project Jasper County, Iowa, Flooding

19. 2011 Project Alabama, Tornado

20. 2011 Project St. Louis, MO, Tornado

21. 2011 Project Springfield, MI, Tornado

22. 2011 Project Minot, ND, Flooding

23. 2011 Project Catskills, NY, Hurricane

26. 2012 Project Morgan County, KY, Tornado

27. 2012 Project Duluth, MN, Flooding

28. 2012 Project MS Gulf Coast, Hurricane

29. 2012 Project Staten Island, Superstorm Sandy

30. 2012 Project Long Island Response, Superstorm Sandy

32. 2013 Project Moore Response, OK, Tornado

33. 2013 Project Long Island Rebuild, Superstorm Sandy

34. 2013 Project Colorado Response, Flooding

35. 2013 Project Staten Island Rebuild, Superstorm Sandy

36. 2013 Project Central Illinois Response, Tornado

39. 2014 Project Mayflower Response, Arkansas, Tornado

40. 2014 Project Itawamba Response, Mississippi, Tornado

42. 2014 Project Colorado Rebuild, Flooding

43. 2014 Project Pilger Response, Tornado

44. 2014 Project Hawaii Response, Tropical Storm

45. 2014 Project Detroit Response, Flooding

47. 2015 Project Boston Response, Snow Removal

49. 2015 Project Brooklyn Rebuild, Superstorm Sandy

51. 2015 Project Detroit Rebuild, Flooding

53. 2015 Project Texas Response, Flooding

54. 2015 Project Kentucky Response, Flooding

Meet the People Behind the Stories

Sara Bareilles, Grammy-award nominated singer and songwriter. Volunteer: Project Tohoku, with her tour group. Produced a documentary benefitting All Hands Volunteers and used social media to help AHV win a much-needed Toyota truck.

Gay Campbell, fine art photographer; devoted grandmother; primary supporter of All Hands since its creation. Volunteer: Biloxi (three times), Philippines (four times), Peru, Bangladesh, Indonesia, Haiti (twice), Japan, Long Beach, and Colorado.

Stefanie Chang, Master of Law and Diplomacy, Tufts Fletcher School. Volunteer: Biloxi and Indonesia. Core AHV staff member on all international projects from 2007 to 2011. First ever AHV Project Director. AHV board member since 2012.

Sarah Comerford, Grants Administrator, Karakin Foundation. Volunteer: Detroit. Donor: Assisted with operational funds, purchase of mobile command center, and establishment of a rapid response fund for small-scale disasters.

Ian D'Arcy, British advertising executive and avid sailor. Volunteer: Peru, Bangladesh, Indonesia, Haiti, New York, and the Philippines. Launched All Hands UK to support donors and volunteers. Major donor and fund-raiser, and AHV board member.

Greg Dietrich, IT Specialist at Credit Suisse. Led teams from Credit Suisse to work on NYC area projects. Arranged a Credit Suisse-sponsored laptop donation program to schools and communities where AHV was working.

Bill Driscoll, Executive Director at Nechama and Interim CEO at NVOAD, the national volunteer organization active in disasters. Volunteer: Biloxi (where he met his current wife, volunteer and Communications Director Beca Howard). First AHV Domestic Operations Director serving on many projects from 2008 to 2012.

Jo-Ann Driscoll, ever-cheerful volunteer. With her husband, Dave, volunteered on many AHV projects in Biloxi and around the world before David's untimely death in 2012. (David is sorely missed.) Jo-Ann provided administrative support in the early days, and provides encouragement forever.

 **Erik Dyson,** Executive Director of All Hands Volunteers since July 2013. Early career experience with Habitat for Humanity International, followed by Harvard MBA. His wife, Debbi, and their daughters Jackie and Abby are members of the All Hands volunteer community.

 **Jack Ferrebee,** Lawyer. Volunteer: Haiti (twice) and New York (a few times). Early AHV "in-house counsel." AHV board member and secretary.

 **Atsuko Fish,** Director, Fish Foundation. Founded the Japan Disaster Relief Fund after the 2011 tsunami and helped launch Project Tohoku with a generous grant. With daughter, Emily, traveled to our project in Ofunato and started sustained assistance to that region.

 **Eric Gebaide,** Investment Banker, Innovation Advisors. Enthusiastic supporter of AHV through sponsored events and fund-raising. Very active volunteer including Biloxi, Iowa, Haiti, and Super Storm Sandy projects, bringing "whole family engagement." Board member since 2010.

 **Sue Glassnor,** "Most Consistent Volunteer." Volunteer: Served on more than twenty projects, both domestic and international, becoming a trusted face in early needs assessment. In addition to her family of many children, both biological and fostered, Sue has made All Hands her extended family.

Adam Haber, business executive, investor, and restaurateur. Along with his wife, Renee, he was an active donor and volunteer in Cedar Rapids, Haiti, and Long Island. Board advisor in Biloxi (Hurricane Katrina) and now board member.

Jeremey Horan, Early volunteer: Biloxi. Project director: Haiti. Operations director for multiple projects. Married to All Hands Volunteer Christina Buchner.

Tom Jardim, Architect. Volunteer: Haiti. Led school construction project that completed twenty schools. Project coordinator for local volunteer program.

April (Nizlek) Jelinek, Long-term volunteer: Indonesia and Haiti. Within thirteen months in Haiti, April managed the rubble and demo work and site evaluations, made the volunteer work-for-the-day schedules and co-ran the biosand water filter project. Married to All Hands Volunteer Michal.

Michal Jelinek, PhD Acoustics. Volunteer: Haiti (twice). "Carpenter, tool manager, breakfast maker, coffee maker, two-pancakes-per-person enforcer, manager of base security, waste and recycling manager, and doer of tons of other less interesting things." Married to All Hands Volunteer April.

 **Bruce Jones,** owner and operator of Milestone Golf Course, in upstate New York, which hosts a yearly tournament to benefit AHV. Volunteer: Thailand (built housing for two camps in Kamala); volunteer/crew leader in Mississippi, Haiti (twice), Philippines (three times), and Staten Island. "I am proud of this organization and so honored to have witnessed its growth. I am even more honored to be part of it."

 **Lee Keet,** business executive, Adirondacks devotee, philanthropist, part-time Parisian. Very early-stage moral supporter, donor, and funder of a challenge grant that was crucial to help build the AHV endowment. Volunteer with wife, Nancy, in Peru. "In Pisco, I was the 'engineer' for a school we were rebuilding but, in fact, I only ended up building a bathroom for the school and helping to make sure that a roof tied the whole school together."

 **Andrew Kerr,** Director of Development, Carolina for Kibera (NGO). Started as a volunteer in Cedar Rapids and quickly became a project coordinator. Hired to be the AHV fund-raiser, then became director of development until December 2012. Remains an active donor.

 **Neil Lawson,** builder. Multi-project, long-term volunteer: Peru, Haiti (twice), Japan (field coordinator), USA (six times), and Philippines (twice). Project coordinator for Itawamba, Mississippi. Married to All Hands Volunteer Coordinator, Jess Thompson.

 **Diana Manilla,** Information Officer, *Médecins Sans Frontières* (Doctors Without Borders); Haiti. Former Field Manager; Save the Children, Central Africa Republic. Volunteer: Haiti. Quickly became staff member as Cash for Work Project Coordinator, Hygiene Promotion Project Coordinator, and Associate Project Director. Earned Masters in Public Health, 2013.

 **Becci Manson,** photo retoucher and TED Talk star (her TED talk has more than 700,000 views). Volunteer: Haiti and Japan, Long Beach, and Staten Island. In Tohoku, Becci created the Photo Rescue Project. Donor and fund-raiser since 2010.

 **Mike McQueeney,** founder of Summer Street Capital. AHV board member and Chair of Development Committee. Sponsored multiple Buffalo, New York, fund-raising events. Volunteer: Haiti and New York, with his family.

 **Darius Monsef,** tech startup entrepreneur: ColorLovers/ CreativeMarket (sold to Autodesk), FanHandle CEO. Co-founded All Hands with David Campbell in 2005. First operations director (2005 to 2007) in USA, Philippines, Peru. Continuing volunteer. All Hands Volunteers board member.

 **Mike Pehl,** partner, North Bridge Growth Equity. Volunteer: Haiti, with college-age son and daughter. The impact of this experience led to him becoming a board member and key donor.

 **Paul Raddant,** Director of International Recovery and Rebuild for AHV. Volunteer: Haiti (three times), working on school rebuild project, became construction supervisor and construction coordinator; Philippines (two times) as program coordinator then program manager; first project director, Staten Island. Projects in Nepal and the Philippines.

 **Nick Taranto,** entrepreneur and co-founder of Plated.com. Volunteer: Thailand, Biloxi (brought and led teams from Dartmouth College), Indonesia, Haiti (brought and led teams from Harvard Business School), and Staten Island. All Hands Volunteers board member.

 **Jess Thompson,** All Hands Volunteer Coordinator. Known as "Jess UK," for her British background. Experience on more than twenty projects inspires her to manage communication with thousands of volunteers with an ever-positive attitude. Met Neil Lawson, now her husband, during Haiti project.

 **Marc Young,** All Hands Volunteers Operations Director, 2005; International Operations Director, 2006 to 2013. "Scuba Marc" was the critical element leading All Hands projects and development. From the HODR-Half houses in Bangladesh to the Joint Logistics Base (JLB) in Haiti, Marc led us to new activities with competence and passion.

Acknowledgments

All Hands Volunteers wouldn't exist without the trust of our donors, the efforts of our volunteers, and the acceptance of the communities around the world that we have helped.

My personal journey required the timely support of special friends, the tremendous staff that created the organization, and the unwavering encouragement of my wife, Gay, and my amazing family.

Thank you, from the bottom of my heart.

About the Authors

David Campbell built on a forty-year technology career to become the cofounder and executive director of All Hands Volunteers.

He began his career with IBM in 1963 and then left to join Computer Task Group, eventually serving as President/CEO for most of his twenty-five-year career there. His later positions have included President of BBN Technologies, CEO of Xpedior, and service on ten public company boards of directors. He received the Manhattan Institute award for Social Entrepreneurship in 2013, and the Symetra Purpose Prize from Encore.org in 2014.

Campbell, originally from Buffalo, New York, earned a bachelor of science in mathematics and a master of science from SUNY-Buffalo, where he has served as a trustee. He has an honorary doctorate from Niagara University, where he is a trustee emeritus.

Catherine Fredman has collaborated on best-selling management strategy books as well as memoirs by Andy Grove (*Only the Paranoid Survive* and *Swimming Across*), Michael Dell (*Direct from Dell* and *The Dell-Lieberman Family Memoir*), and Maria Bartiromo (*Use the News*), and Gideon Gartner (*@Gartner*), among others. She lives in New York City, where she volunteers as a Central Park tour guide and has swum around the Statue of Liberty.

CPSIA information can be obtained at www.ICGtesting.com
Printed in the USA
LVOW06s1032131015

458055LV00003B/80/P